D0064994

Managing in Times of Radical Change

Managing in Times of Radical Change

John J. Fendrock

American Management Association

To my former co-workers
at Avion Electronics, Inc.,
who,
enduring twelve years of trial and error
while I learned my trade,
contributed much to my education
as a manager

© American Management Association, Inc., 1971.
All rights reserved. Printed in the United States of America.

This publication may not be reproduced, stored in a retrieval system,
or transmitted in whole or in part, in any form or by any means,
electronic, mechanical, photocopying, recording, or otherwise,
without the prior written permission of the Association.

International standard book number: 0-8144-5262-0
Library of Congress catalog card number: 75-154686

FIRST PRINTING

Preface

Movements have begun today which will result in a world quite different from the one we live in. Much of what had been taken for granted is being questioned and ridiculed, and an uncertainty exists where confidence once prevailed. A new social consciousness has emerged that demands improved living conditions for all people. This nation must become better environmentally, socially, and economically, or the discontent that has revealed itself may result in the destruction of all that has been painfully built over the centuries.

To allow others to dictate what will be done in accommodating business and industry to the needs of the evolving society would be a copout by managers. They know *what* must be done; *how* to get it done must still be worked out. Hackneyed approaches will not suffice; change is coming, and imagination will be needed to develop the innovations that solve the problems besetting industry.

In themselves, the ideas in this book are not intended to be answers to the problems discussed. They are proposed as approaches that might be taken, in conjunction with other, perhaps more daring measures, to help executives prevent a further erosion of their authority by government and nonbusiness groups. Instead of being instigators of change, businessmen are becoming instruments carrying out policies developed by others. The argument of this book is that these roles must be reversed—that managers need to assume a more active and creative role in attacking the ills afflicting business and, as a consequence, society.

The theme is that managers must recognize the world outside their offices and respond to the challenges being thrown their way. They must become aware of the changes occurring in managerial techniques and of the restlessness these are causing within their own ranks. They must find ways to keep executives interested in their jobs, to inspire new managers with enthusiasm, and to converse unemotionally with dissatisfied young people. Society demands that business attend to its needs, or it will impose its will on businessmen. Managers must learn to communicate, with each other and with people who are not immersed in the business world. They must become integrated into the life of their communities, or they will be ignored as the narrow-minded, uncultured workers of society. The problems discussed here are the ones that the author feels will be most pressing in this decade, and the ideas expressed are intended to stimulate the reader to formulate far more imaginative solutions of his own to the ills of management.

Many people contributed to this book over the years. The author's exchanges with managers, politicians, social workers, young people and elderly ones, whites and nonwhites, women employees and wives of managers—all helped develop the themes expressed. Particular recognition must be extended to some people: To Jack Records, group vice president of General Signal Corporation, Inc., Terrance A. Flannagan, president of Terrance Flannagan Associates, and Dr. Matthew Radom, former chairman of the management division, Rutgers University (now on leave as a consultant to Israel), sincere thanks for their helpful suggestions and criticisms. To Vivian Charles and Pauline Shipker I am grateful for perceptive observations on career women and, in Miss Shipker's case, for untiring efforts to decipher the worst handwriting in the world. Certainly this book could not have been written without the wonderful cooperation of my wife Lillian and of John, Charles, and Bernadette, who learned to live with their favorite pop and rock music played decibels lower than *they* enjoy it in deference to their father, the part-time author.

While he gratefully acknowledges the assistance of others, the author accepts full responsibility for the ideas, proposals, observations, and conclusions expressed.

John J. Fendrock

Contents

1

An Angry Society— Management Under Fire

THE once-confident American society has been infected with an illness that is still to be diagnosed. Its symptoms are discontent, distrust, aggressiveness, and ennui. The social body of America had labored long and hard to develop health and well-being, and no effort had been spared to keep it in good condition. But for some unknown reason, despite that hard and even loving work, society has been attacked by malaise and now finds itself battling to preserve what was so arduously built.

There are many who feel that this truly wonderful political creation is doomed. Others think that the attack of fever is part of the American growth process and will be eliminated in the usual orderly way. Still others contend that our society, while basically healthy, must be restudied to discover what is wrong. They maintain that whatever gave America brain fever cannot be ignored, because it may prove overpowering for even the strongest of constitutions.

Although it is impossible to ascertain who is correct in

these contradictory analyses, everyone agrees that whatever happens, America will never be the same again. And since the analyses deal only with the symptoms while the causes remain elusive, frustration is becoming a permanent American state of mind. Because of our feeling of helplessness, a dangerous anger has arisen among us. Even if the disease itself is discovered and eventually cured, this anger may have made whatever is left to us worthless.

Apart from our role as citizens, we should be very much concerned because a large part of that anger is being directed at us as users of the country's resources. While this is not the first time that management has been under criticism, there is something special about what is happening today. It is the accusation that the formerly heralded accomplishments of American business and industry are a sham—that, in fact, instead of being praised for what they have done and are doing, managers should be censured and their activities curtailed or even abolished.

Why have large numbers of Americans turned from a rather self-satisfied group into an angry mob, dissatisfied with the "establishment" and with managers, the providers of their material well-being? A brief review of the history of this about-face may demonstrate that it is not possible to live in seclusion, ignoring what is taking place in community life, and may illustrate why business, which did this for so long, now finds its managers under fire.

From New Frontier to National Frustration

It is only a few short years since ours was called the complacent generation. College students were berated for their lack of interest in affairs on- or off-campus; they only studied. The Eisenhower years were termed a period of national lugubriousness. Observers feared the country might be losing its drive and enthusiasm for change and progress.

The short Kennedy period ushered in an era of international tension, which was relieved without upsetting the confidence of the people in their leaders. And although some disturbances began to appear at home, serious outbreaks were avoided through rhetoric and timely action. The glitter, youth, and energy of America's First Family captivated all segments of society. The change from the paternalistic years of President Eisenhower to the exuberant time of President Kennedy was graceful but dramatic.

Throughout the world America was seen as a newly progressive, flexible nation whose former self-righteousness was being cast aside. The Bay of Pigs demonstrated to Americans the futility of acting independently of world opinion; even our friends abroad were disturbed by the deceit reflected in Adlai Stevenson's alibis in the United Nations, apparently given in ignorance of an invasion that had been planned in close secrecy. The Cuban missile crisis then showed the world how fragile is the barrier that holds back the destructive power of nuclear warfare. It also told enemy and friend that a maturity had developed in America, that America's leaders had eschewed recklessness and were capable of sober judgment and action during critical periods. A new respect for this country emerged abroad, while self-confidence grew at home. The world had seen the greatest nation on earth back down from an ill-conceived venture in response to indignant international public opinion. It had also watched in horrid fascination as that nation looked down the barrel of nuclear death and did not waver. America had shown it could suffer a major wound without fatal consequences. Despite the hurt it had received in Cuba with the ill-conceived and -conducted invasion, the country was still capable of meeting its archenemy in direct nuclear confrontation, controlling its passions, and maintaining honor, integrity, and national well-being.

Within the nation, the young leader responded to the unrest that began to appear in the areas of civil rights and poverty. With a vigor that may have been more show than accomplishment, he managed to keep the forces being generated in pockets of discontent effectively below the explosion point. Perhaps an astute observer might have recognized that the veneer of glamour his response cast over the ugliness that existed in these areas would not be strong enough in the long run to confine the building pressures. It is possible that they could have been vented somehow, but what was done proved inadequate in the light of events.

A lone gunman in Dallas killed a president.

He also killed the dream of millions of Americans.

Five years later, Martin Luther King and Robert Kennedy followed President John Kennedy in the sights of assassins' guns.

The senseless killings did more than snuff out the lives of three men. Coupled with the murders of a number of less known people, they jolted the country, which had been basking in a feeling of renewed purpose and direction, out of its euphoria. The promise of a new voyage was over, and an aimlessness replaced it.

The frantic efforts of President Lyndon B. Johnson to cancel years of neglect in the fields of civil rights and poverty were useless. Showing more valiance than another might have under the circumstances, he fostered and enforced legislation that was against his own regional principles and tried to stem the onrushing tide of social unrest. Reacting to what he thought was the will of the American people, he took the advice of the brilliant men around him, their arguments supported with public opinion polls, and pursued a ruinous course in Vietnam.

Abroad, the North Vietnamese began to seriously threaten South Vietnam at a time when America was least able to act rationally. This country became involved in a conflict that was contrary to the counsel of most military and diplomatic advisory groups. A land war in the jungles of Asia against an unfriendly peasant population could not be won. But despite repeated assertions to the contrary, America found itself sinking faster and faster into the quicksand of a conflict it did not want, could not win, yet seemed unable to avoid. America's prestige plummeted. Formerly friendly nations became sanctuaries for deserters from her armies. Other countries, trying hard to stand by a respected and loved ally, criticized her to the point where relationships which extended back to the founding of the republic were threatened. Less charitable nations accused the United States of murder and willful destruction of Vietnam under the guise of saving it. The best intentions of many men were shattered as what promised to be a short-lived police action turned into a nightmare of war that lasted longer than any other in American history.

The delicate balance in this country between restive groups and a government attempting to respond to their wants was weakened by the deaths of a number of young leaders on both sides, and was completely upset by the action in South Vietnam. Civil rights disorders erupted in the cities. Americans now knew firsthand what destruction and violent death were like. Unprepared for what was happening, police and peace-keeping officers sometimes overreacted.

The uncertainty abroad was now brought home. Emotions and objectives became confused as groups with unrelated goals intermixed in demonstrating, defying, and destroying. Determined to do something about the causes of discontent, numbers of well-meaning, law-abiding people intermingled with trouble-making, destructive lawbreakers whose goal was chaos and anarchy. Groups with this unnatural combination of interests and with no defined common objective descended upon the Democratic Convention in Chicago determined to do something. What it was no one, including themselves, knew. In three days the city went through a period of disgraceful conduct, on the part of law officers as well as confused people, that left the entire country emotionally exhausted. During the selection of a candidate for its highest office, a large number of people, including those who presumably were the people's protectors, exhibited the worst of their natures. The reaction against the established government reached its climax in the violent days of Chicago.

While the causes of the country's illness remained as elusive as ever, no effort was spared in attempting to detect them. Elected officials received their share of criticism, one result of which was the decision of President Johnson not to run for another term in office.

President Richard M. Nixon took over a country that no longer placed faith in its leaders. The unexpected length of the Asian conflict was playing havoc with the nation's economy, for the large military spending was coupled with a previously made space commitment. Some economists prophesied danger if inflation were allowed to continue at its accelerating pace, but their warnings went unheeded.

The country drifted into a gentle but steady recession that affected white collar workers as well as blue. The stock market reacted in a series of violent drops. The president, again convinced that he had to follow the recommendations of trusted advisers, expanded the Asian conflict by ordering a brief invasion of Cambodia.

The response of civic protesters and students was quick and emotional. Angry groups staged protests and rallies. On college campuses, classes were suspended. With the conditions that prevailed, all this could not take place without violence. From Harvard and Yale to Berkeley and San Francisco, students who felt betrayed at the polls by their elders and ignored by their legislators erupted in mob action. They demonstrated and destroyed, showing irreverence for all that had been considered sacred since the founding of higher education in America. They put the university community on the defensive, calling it a tool of the establishment, of the reactionary forces leading the country to disaster.

As if to indicate the profundity of the crisis, the culmination of these student activities occurred in the heart of America. The killing of four uninvolved, onlooking students at Kent University brought about a national trauma. Further demonstrations broke out, from marching hard-hats in Wall Street to fire bombings of the Bank of America in San Francisco. And while other mindless bombings took place, while smaller protest actions were staged, the country lay back, tending the deep wounds it had suffered.

Signs of Something Wrong

Americans feel that despite its faults, this is the most perfect system of government which ever existed. Yet most also agree that the sudden and unexpected violence throughout the land is a sign of something basically wrong. The extent of this violence, and its penetration into so many groups in the country, indicates that there have been inequities of long standing which affect many people.

While America was never in a position to trumpet its advances in the field of civil rights, there was no lack of time spent in demonstrating good intentions. The black entertainer and sports star received their share of publicity, and were used as examples of what could be done by blacks who have what it takes and play according to the white man's rules. This well-meant but totally inadequate effort toward racial economic equalization was described by black men as nothing more than white man's hypocrisy. The civil disturbances that erupted across the nation revealed the discontent that existed. Local, state, and federal government was told in charcoal messages, illuminated by the flames from Newark, Detroit, and Watts, that it had failed a large segment of society.

As for the American woman, once she had been given the right to vote the gate to political and economic freedom in this country was open to her. For a long time, however, her attention was diverted from this area with beauty pageants, fashion parades, and pancake races. Occasionally a woman politician, scientist, writer, or sportswoman made the front pages of the newspaper, but she was looked upon as an exception. Today the truly emancipated woman refuses to accept this concept of "equality" of the sexes, and she is prepared to change things.

One measure of a society is the way it handles its offspring. Judging by the treatment American children receive, ours is the most advanced, progressive, and enlightened culture that ever existed. Our children are pampered and coddled. Their very wishes become parental commands, and they are given everything that money can buy. Instead of being grateful, however, they throw this very kindness and concern back at the older generation with the accusation that these are nothing more than a cover-up for parental inadequacies. No longer are these children, now that they are students in high school and college, the silent, gracious, grateful offspring they were expected to become. With a crudeness that shocks parents and teachers alike, they use four-letter words to describe what they think of the world that was built for them, and they show a destructive side that was assumed to have disappeared with their last infant tantrum. Parents are told that they have lost the image of dispensers of truth; educators are given notice that their students can no longer be taken for granted.

The pride that Americans once felt on the Fourth of July or at the raising of the flag, the thrill that came when the National Anthem was sung and military bands marched, the resounding recitation of our might that gave a sense of national unity and strength—all these have taken on a different meaning because of Vietnam. Americans were once proud that the country had never lost a war. Today, many feel that we have suffered our first defeat, a military defeat stemming from a political mistake, and that the sooner we accept and acknowledge this fact the better we will be as a nation. For many Americans those former spine-tingling sensations of patriotism have been replaced by tremors of shame for our Asian misadventure.

Religious institutions have also been rocked as the deep-seated frustrations of some of their members came to the surface. Once-revered authority has been questioned and long-standing rules and customs challenged. The afterlife has been forgotten as today's needs are pursued. Cherished beliefs and customs have been revised or eliminated in an effort to keep abreast of the changing world.

The philosophers and moralists who defend gradual reform have been brushed aside by those who insist upon revolution rather than evolution. Overpopulation—unwanted children—freedom of expression which demands that all be shown, said, and seen—the right to escape into drug-induced flights from reality—all are considered problems of such urgency that time cannot be wasted in debating them. Thousands of years of accumulated social conventions have been upset in the space of a decade, and new ways of living and acting and dying have taken over.

It was inevitable that during this time of self-analysis and uncertainty, the materialistic way of life, which made ours the most affluent society in history, should come under scrutiny. In the process the results of a century and a half of accumulated effort to produce this goods-oriented society became only too apparent.

The Work of the Past

When the country was young, the sight of a steam locomotive belching clouds of black smoke was a source of pride, a symbol of strength and progress. The automobile with its chrome and roar was the American version of the Latin's *machismo*—his manhood. The slivers of steel and ribbons of concrete that tied cities together were modern trails uniting a nation. And people ran out of their houses to wave when they heard the hum of an airplane.

In those days, telephone poles and strings of electric lines were a barometer of a town's growth: the more densely cluttered the space above the street, the more prosperous the community. Civic organizations vied with each other in luring industry to their towns. No thought was given to the question of pollution; everyone knew that a new industry meant lower taxes and increased spending power.

As the age of inventions progressed, chemists outdid themselves in developing useful products: clear plastics, unbreakable packages, throwaway containers, insecticides that last for years, gasolines that give more mileage at higher speeds, additives that preserve foods from discoloration and decay. Such products were hailed as milestones in man's struggle against an unfriendly nature. By creating new alloys, metallurgists produced thin, strong metals that had many applications: they were used to build automobiles that proved relatively inexpensive yet relatively reliable, and that did not outlast their appeal; they were made into structural members that allowed the imagination of architects to soar. Engineers dreamed up wonder after wonder: their laboratories turned out dishwashers, electric typewriters, clothes driers, electric can openers, air conditioners, dehumidifiers, electric knives, electric toothbrushes, electric shoeshine kits, jet airplanes, television, and refrigerator-freezers.

Who would have thought that in time the men and women who invested, produced, and distributed these magnificent accouterments of modern living would be vilified as defilers of the environment, destroyers of our heritage, and purveyors of filth and trash?

It might be argued that many of the things that are called cheap, ugly, and harmful were the work of the past—that today's industrial establishment is not responsible for them. Or it could be said that these things are allowed to continue in existence because the great majority demand them. Certainly it can be proved that if the polluting automobile, locomotive, and airplane and their unsightly highways, tracks, and airports were eliminated, the nation would revert to a primitive state. Simple economics demonstrate that the country could not exist if all ugly and contaminating industrial activity were stopped. Furthermore, our vast population obviously could not be fed without cans and plastic containers for distributing food. And everyone realizes that the channeling of human waste into streams and rivers could not be suddenly stopped without creating a greater health and sanitary problem than now exists.

Though all this may be true, it has little relevance for our restless society in its ugly mood. Tomorrow does not exist for a large segment of the population. Changes must be made *now*—today—and hang the consequences.

The Glories of Free Enterprise

Since it is American industry that has been responsible for the flood of products sold to the public, the industrialist bears a major part of the criticism for the ugliness that resulted from their use. The flow of accusations has been continuous, and broader in scope than might have been expected. Managers and businessmen have been criticized for insufficient concern with such areas as product quality and value, the needs of minority groups, pollution control, women's rights, productive effort, improvements in civic government, and utilization of human resources.

A few years ago, accusations that were made against a company's practices were pursued in a legal framework which was generally favorable to business. An antitrust action, for example, or a price-fixing complaint was brought into court and settled there. The corporation or some of its executives might be penalized, and the community might be shocked by the fraudulent practices which had been revealed.

Once the penalty had been paid, however, it was felt that justice had been served. Today this is changed. The past practices of companies and industries are under scrutiny, present activities are constantly questioned, and future plans are evaluated by an inquisitive society. And they are measured against yardsticks that are quite different from any used before.

It had been held that a company was free to do what was necessary to produce a profit so long as it did not violate an existing law. The lure of profits encouraged the daring; to succeed was to reap handsome rewards for taking risks. With this free-wheeling enterprise, the country grew and prospered. Not only did the risk taker, the investor, benefit, but those who worked for him shared in his good fortune through continued employment and rising wages as the business expanded.

Since the worker received pay for his work, the scale was balanced each week when he was handed his paycheck. He gave, and he received for what he gave. Not so the owners. They gambled constantly against some unforeseen event that could wipe out their investment. Whether it was the kerosene lamp manufacturer who was displaced by the electric light, or the buggy shop that was made obsolete by the automobile, they took special risks. Inevitably the owner was considered as performing a special function in the growing economy. It was apparent that this system's benefits to society were great, since free enterprise provided employment and material well-being for its members. These were made available with as little interference from the government as possible. The least government was the best, and industry, by providing jobs and salaries, was helping democracy remain pure.

It was natural to extend this logic to the precept that what was good for the company was good for the country. The concept of free enterprise took on the appearance of dogma. Any attempt to regulate or control industrial activity, whether in respect to size, degree of competition, product quality or price, treatment of workers or their efforts to organize, safety or health conditions, or abuse of national resources was immediately met with warnings of the impending destruction of the system and the rise of socialism. The American experiment, so obviously successful yet so little understood, was thought to be somewhat like a delicate mechanism. Any tampering with the movements might easily throw it off balance, and the long-run trend of benefits might lose momentum.

Champions of free enterprise cited many examples to illustrate the dangers of "socialistic" interference with an economy. They pointed to the continuing economic crises in Europe, which were accompanied by constant threats of devaluation, restricted export of money, curtailed consumer buying, and high taxes. These problems, they claimed, could only be attributed to government interference with the economy. What the critics overlooked was that the highly successful industrial systems of Germany, Italy, the Scandinavian countries, and Japan were tightly controlled. Moreover, if the apparently economically sick countries were objectively examined, patterns could be discerned that indicated a far more complex set of conditions than the original simple conclusion suggested.

A harsh judgment of what has happened over the course of American industrial expansion has led some to conclude that the free enterprise system was a monster which devoured those who served it. Yet if it did treat some members of society harshly, most people at the time felt that this was done not arbitrarily but in accordance with the rough laws of nature. Survival of the fittest and natural selection were considered to be applicable in the economic world as well as in the natural state. And like the glories of the natural world, the wonders of America's growth and well-being were believed to result from this severe but just law. Certainly none can deny that American society gained overwhelmingly from the free enterprise approach.

It was therefore with great reluctance that legislation was gradually passed governing worker safety, hours of employment, Social Security, unemployment benefits, the right to unionize, and medical care. Businessmen were shocked when antitrust laws were introduced, when pure food and drug laws were enacted, when quality standards were imposed on industry. These and a host of other laws that were passed encroaching upon the rights of managers were viewed as grave threats to the American way of life. Slowly the business world accommodated to the interfering legislation, sometimes complying with it, sometimes finding legal ways to evade it.

Managers knew that their first responsibility was to the owners—the stockholders. The public and the government agreed. The manager worked diligently to maximize profits, giving the owner the greatest possible return on his money, and the manager in turn received incentive compensation based on the growth of the owner's investment. It seemed reasonable to assume that if all members of society were to become stockholders, the widespread ownership of companies would stimulate everyone to work harder and, perhaps, show less interest in curtailing the power of management. With industry's encouragement, the public became partners of industry through outright purchase of stock, mutual funds, invested money from union pensions, company-sponsored stock purchase plans, and stock bonuses. A large segment of the American people thus found themselves with a direct interest in the profitable operation of American business.

New Yardsticks

With an economic base so wide, it was difficult to anticipate disaffection with companies and their managers. The eagerness shown by the public to invest seemed to indicate overwhelming confidence in the way managers were doing their jobs. It was true that an occasional disturbing incident might arise: a case of price-fixing by some of the most respected members of the industrial community, or a company's significant loss due to mismanagement, or a disaster caused by inadequate safety precautions, or a company's decision to move and abandon long-term employees. These events, however, produced nothing more than a ripple on the surface of the business waters. The growth and expansion of industry were too swift, the innovations and discoveries too dazzling, the well-being and contentment of society simply too great.

Suddenly this complacency was shaken. As convulsion after agonizing convulsion upset the nation's confidence, the searching eye of the discontented investigator, self-appointed or group-sponsored, soon lit on the company and its managers.

The excuse that today's management cannot be held accountable for its predecessors' mistakes was not accepted.

The concept that management's only responsibility is to produce profits was brushed aside as a sophistry.

The argument that the company might be bankrupted by undertaking costly improvements to reduce pollution was viewed as evidence of managerial incompetence.

Management's fear of the high cost of social involvement was taken as proof of the inadequacy of free competition.

The insistence of many companies that they had a civic obligation to produce goods needed by the military was considered unpatriotic.

The whole fabric of corporate cloth that had been woven so carefully was being torn to shreds. Managers were frustrated in carrying out their work. They were at a loss for ways to cope with the new environment they found themselves working and living in.

Adding to the confusion were a number of disturbing developments in the business world. Caught up in the rapid events, many companies were forced to sit in the spotlight of publicity when they would have preferred not to. The picture they presented to the public and to managers themselves was less than reassuring; frequently the giants of American business and industry were in a weak and defensive position.

The chairman of the board of General Motors, in an appearance before a Senate investigating committee, apologized to an unknown lawyer for the actions of his company, which had hired a group of investigators to look into the lawyer's personal life for something that could be used to discredit him. The lawyer, who did not approve of the quality of a car sold by General Motors, had put his doubts into a best-selling book attacking automobile companies and claiming that they had a callous disregard for people's safety.

The president of Dow Chemical undertook a series of speaking engagements at campuses throughout the country. His purpose was not to sell products or to try and interest the abusive students in working for his company. Rather, he was attempting to bridge the gap between the campus and business in general—to recreate the atmosphere of harmony that had previously existed between the aspiring student and the potential employer.

National Guardsmen stood duty at various branches of the Bank of America, the largest in the United States. After having burned one building, students were threatening others in a show of displeasure with the material embodiment of the establishment in California.

Newsweek, a magazine that dutifully reported discontent and disruptions, found itself the target of demonstrations by its own female employees. They confronted management with a sit-in to protest what they felt was its failure to treat women on an equal footing with men.

Consolidated Edison of New York was repeatedly forced to postpone plans for a nuclear power plant owing to objections from lovers of nature, who feared destruction of the fish in the rivers and of the beauty of the entire Hudson Palisades. Under pressure from the conservationists, legislators formed investigating committees while construction plans gathered dust and the threat of power failure grew.

Union Oil Company, as a result of an oil leak in one of its offshore wells, became engaged in a public relations battle with citizens on the California coast. Through editorial comment, speakers' remarks, and letters to the papers and magazines, the residents were able to force a temporary stop in oil drilling in the area while the procedures for all offshore oil exploration were reviewed.

Lockheed Aircraft Corporation held its annual meeting in a well-guarded hangar in an effort to prevent interruptions and demonstrations by peace groups protesting Lockheed's war production.

Penn Central Transportation Company, the largest railroad in the world, was forced into bankruptcy amid charges of mismanagement, misinformation to the public, and abuse of inside information in stock transactions. The former managers of the company claimed that it was impossible to run a business so hobbled with government red tape and regulatory handcuffs.

As they instituted programs to train the underprivileged, the four major automobile manufacturers acknowledged a responsibility to help rectify the imbalance in opportunities between white and Negro applicants.

Construction and trade unions, while maintaining a tight grip on the hiring practices of employers, worked toward creating equal opportunities for those not fortunate enough to have entry into their unions through normal channels.

A Reconciliation with Society

That there is conflict between the new social yardsticks and the traditional practices of business management is no longer questioned. That some of the resulting problems are great and complex is apparent from the reactions of companies and their managers. But whether management's response to the crisis has been serious enough, imaginative enough, and broad enough is being questioned by a restless society. If management's accusers decide that it is producing only a token response, there may be increasing demands that the responsibility for reform be taken out of the hands of businessmen.

Many of the options for corrective action that were once open to managers have been closed by their slowness and reluctance to accept the initiative. This unwillingness is not difficult to understand. No manager receives a mandate from owners to spend the company's money on upgrading the environment, eliminating pollution, rectifying social inequities, championing the rights of women, or satisfying protest marchers.

It is not surprising, then, that many managers need to have a law passed ordering them to correct a deplorable condition before they feel justified in spending company funds. The legal threat absolves them from the charge of forsaking their first objective, the maximization of profit. But unless business managers can persuade their owners to relinquish the short-term profit for the long-term gain, the response of business to the social problems facing it will be dictated by others. Laws will be passed outlining what must or must not be done by business, and the area of managerial decision making will be progressively restricted. Unless management is prepared to abdicate responsibility for corrective action, it is imperative that managers undertake to define for their owners, the stockholders, courses of action that will more than satisfy the wants of society.

It will take strong men to tell owners that what was done in the past to produce returns must now be changed. It will take even stronger men to relate the unhappy facts about the reduction in immediate profits that these changes will bring. But if projects for social gain are undertaken with wisdom, it should be possible to persuade legislators to provide tax benefits in compensation. Careful planning and budgeting of socially desirable projects could also help companies avoid major impacts on equity returns. With business taking the lead in developing ideas and generating plans, the less fortunate companies could receive financial assistance through industrywide insurance from sinking funds for use on socially needed projects.

What is proposed is that business, through its managers, undertake a reconciliation with society. In the past they have shown a magnificent ability to anticipate the material wants of the people for whom they produced goods and services. It is now important that they use their talent and ingenuity to satisfy the nonmaterial wants of the same people. They can do it if they accept the role of leadership in industrial-social reform and develop the plans that will resolve the present conflict. But if managers insist on defending the status quo and acting only on instigation from others, they will relinquish to others the responsibility of defining the future relationship between business and society.

It is the thesis of this book that today's managers can and will accept the challenge that has been presented to them by people who are upset at what they see in commercial life. It follows that as a result of this commitment, American industry and business will remain the freest and the most productive anywhere in the world.

2

Managers as
Social Activists

THAT's not my problem!

This phrase used by a subordinate causes more gnashing of teeth among managers than any other in the language. Yet many executives excuse themselves in the same words when they are charged with indifference toward socio-industrial problems. Is this excuse any more valid in the larger context than in the smaller? Certainly not when the manager is responsible for a condition that creates a social nuisance or danger. Still, the continuing conflict on these problems between well-intentioned businessmen and their adversaries attests to the inability or unwillingness of managers to accept responsibility for what they are accused of doing.

It would be simplistic to conclude that the head of a paper company which spews sulfurous fumes over a city does not know that his plant is contaminating the air.

The airline official who looks at one of his jet aircraft blowing streamers of black smoke is not blind.

Metal processing managers know that a single check of

their waste flow into a river or lake is accurate when it shows mercury being deposited in the water.

Aluminum, tin, glass, and plastic containers, which are so thickly distributed over our highways, forests, and parks that they have become a symbol of our civilization, look no better to their producers than to the rest of us.

Old automobiles, which are abandoned in empty lots, hidden in clumps of trees, dumped in lakes and rivers, piled along busy thoroughfares, forgotten in backyards, and literally disposed of anywhere that desperate people can think of, are seen by their manufacturers as well as by everyone else.

Oil company executives and their teams of geologists know better than any sleuth checking out a leak just where the black goo that contaminates beaches, killing birds and water life, is coming from.

Smoke from a chimney, stench from a chemical plant, and noise from a riveter's hammer hurt the eyes, noses, and ears of their generators as much as those of the public.

The men responsible for deceptive packaging, hidden interest charges, false product claims, unsafe household products, and dangerous children's toys are intelligent people who know the degree to which their goods deviate from the advertised claims.

These and other conditions that are making our environment unhealthy, unpleasant, and, if things continue, unfit for human habitation, are readily identifiable. Their sources are clear, yet they continue. The reason why they have not already been corrected is simply that in our free enterprise system, the job of putting them right could not be specifically assigned to anyone. Hence it was difficult to find anyone charitable enough to assume responsibility.

The paper company that contaminates the air and the waterways spent a considerable amount of money on its plant. Knowing that much water would be needed, it built on a river with more than an adequate flow. Because of the fumes that would pour from the stacks, it submitted plans for approval which conformed to federal, state, and local ordinances. Almost certainly there was overwhelming support from civic bodies, government officials, and the public for this income-producing and tax-paying industry that would be located in their town.

When the jet airplane made its appearance, the streamers of smoke behind it created curving patterns which followed that graceful machine in flight. The black line quickly disappeared, and with it, any thought of its effect on the air.

The reason why industrial plants were often located on riverbanks or lakeshores was that manufacturers wanted an inexpensive way to dispose of wastes. The relatively small amounts of poisons or contaminants dumped into waterways were too insignificant to be worth considering. The bodies of water were so large, the rivers so swift, that reasonable men could not be expected to worry about pollution.

The litter of empty containers and abandoned automobiles spread over the landscape clearly is not the producers' doing. The public obviously prefers to have its countryside, cities, and towns decorated with pop art rather than find other ways to dispose of unwanted junk. Moreover, the consumer happily buys from, borrows from, praises, and keeps in business those companies that deceive and harm him and his family. He will not devote the time or the effort necessary to protect himself, but cheerfully matches his wits against the experts in the marketing world. Again and again he is bested, but he always comes back for more. Clearly he does not feel that the problems of pollution, safety, and ethics are his responsibility.

Where, then, does the responsibility belong for what is happening to our environment? Obviously with the public, with national, state, and local officials, and with industry. The condition that our society finds itself in today is a result of narrow-minded thinking by all these sectors; it is impossible to assign greater blame to one than to the others.

It follows that industry must take steps, independently

and in concert with the other sectors, to resolve the problems. Moreover, if industry does not want to be saddled with a disproportionate share of the financial burden for making improvements, as well as with most of the criticism for the existing problems, it must lead the way in correcting them. While there are areas where industry cannot act alone (and suggested approaches to these will be given later in the chapter), clear avenues are open that management can follow independently.

Management's Stumbling Blocks

The first major obstacle that managers must overcome is that of self-righteousness. They have not been as concerned with what they make, or develop, or sell as they should be, and it is time that they accepted this without becoming defensive about every detail. In a business action which provokes public disapproval, there may be mitigating circumstances that could result in vindication as soon as the circumstances are known. But there is no reason to issue denials to any and all criticism. These are usually followed by belated retractions which sound worse than a clear admission of error in the first place. Managers must learn to deal with the public as they are expected to behave among themselves; they must show intellectual honesty or they will inevitably be exposed.

Second, managers must remove the blinders that permit them to see only the corporate point of view on all subjects. They must recognize that almost everything they do has an impact upon some area of the public sector. In reviewing a corporate proposal, it is as important to consider the social effects of the project as it is to evaluate the effects on an internal department. To ignore either could have serious repercussions and where the public is concerned, these might extend much farther than the specific project. Every action should be appraised to determine if there is a potential conflict between the company's good and society's good; they are not always the same.

Third, managers must learn to live in the precarious world which actually forms the business leader's area of operations, although its existence was not acknowledged until recently. The assumption used to be that the manager existed in a two-dimensional vertical world: Above him were the owners in the form of stockholders, represented by the board of directors. Below him was a large group of employees who served as his muscle in putting the output of his brain to work. Today the model, though it may still be viewed as two-dimensional, has been changed to a horizontal one—a circle with the manager in the center. The owners, government, the public, the company's employees, and associations within the industry are viewed as centrifugal forces tending to pull his authority and effort apart, while thin spokes representing rewards, cooperation, negotiation, and coercion are the centripetal forces holding the moving wheel together. Managers must accept the fact that their comfortable hierarchical world has been reshaped into a far more threatening one. They must learn to live in the total environment surrounding them, or they may be eliminated from their pivotal position by a stronger force in that environment.

The fourth and perhaps most difficult hurdle that managers must overcome is the time-honored theorem that their main goal is to maximize profits. There are a number of complex reasons why a modification of this precept may be essential to American business—and a number of other reasons why it may prove impossible to alter. For a manager, in his capacity as a hired person, to undertake an action aimed at less than maximum profits requires a change of major proportions in the thinking of the investing public, and in the manager himself. No one today expects a manager to correct a pollution problem created by his plant or to decide not to produce a potentially profitable commodity because it may be detrimental to the environment, or to admit that what his company says in an advertisement is not really so. Given our present cultural climate, where people make a neat distinction between themselves as investors and as social beings, such a manager would not represent the stockholders for very long. And just as the stockholders are conditioned to reckon in terms of return on investment, today's managers are not trained to think in terms other than profitability. To assume that either will change overnight is unrealistic.

In a comparable situation, General Douglas MacArthur and the military establishment were thrown into confusion when he was ordered to fight less than a winning war in Korea. Their tradition, their way of life, all the things they believed in were centered on victory in battle. Confronted with the need to give political and diplomatic considerations equal footing with battlefield strategy, he and his advisers were unable to respond. President Truman then made what may turn out to be a trail-blazing decision in exercising civilian authority over the military.

It is possible that a confrontation of such proportions, initiated by some unknown tactician of the business world against the exclusiveness of the profitability yardstick, may be required before industry can give serious attention to social considerations. But there is no real reason for a showdown between stockholders and their managers. Split-second decisions with men's lives in the balance are not involved here; stockholders and managers have time to develop a rapport and an understanding of their mutual objectives.

For example, industry today is receiving severe criticism in areas relating to the environment, to product safety, and to deceptive advertising. What are some of the practical ways for managers to deal with friction concerning these problems, and how can they explain their actions to the owners?

Ecology and the Executive

Managers who are not in some way concerned with problems of environmental quality are in a favored position—or they may be refusing to recognize the fact that they are involved. They might think differently if they were to open their eyes, noses, or ears to the effects of their operations.

The manager must first make a realistic and honest appraisal of his plants and facilities: Are they contributing at all toward despoiling the environment, and if so to what extent? Is industrial waste being discharged into storm or sanitary sewers? (Possibly it was begun at a time when no one thought of making a distinction between various kinds of waste materials.) Do a plant's high-temperature annealing furnaces, which give off practically no smoke, throw invisible nitrides and hydrocarbons into the atmosphere? Does an installation only marginally satisfy regulations governing protective devices, so that slight variations from design conditions can cause an ecological disaster? Is the noise of a factory process far more than a neighboring community should be expected to live with?

If anything in the operation adversely affects the environment, the most naïve policy the company can adopt is to deny or make excuses for it. The manager's job is to know about it, formulate plans for remedying it, calculate the cost, and prepare detailed procedures. He should then present the program to the board of directors so that a decision, based on well-reasoned arguments, can be made either to follow it through or to postpone it.

This action must originate with management because it is impossible for any other group to be familiar enough with what is happening to make a detailed analysis of the problem. Moreover, it is every manager's duty to report situations that might have a detrimental effect upon the company, whether this effect would appear during his tenure or that of his successors. The officers and board of directors who are

confronted in a stockholders' meeting with accusations of environmental damage that they were not even aware of will
look unfavorably upon the executives who failed to keep
them informed. Thus the manager who shows interest in a socially harmful condition may be more practical than altruis-
tic. Just as a manager cannot stand surprises from lower-level
supervisors in the operation of his business, neither can his
own supervisors be left unprepared for a public attack.

If the board of directors approves of a proposed correction
and decides to undertake the changes immediately, community leaders should be given a full disclosure of what it means
to the company, and their concurrence should be secured. A
full disclosure means a complete history of how the condition
came about, why it continued, what can and cannot be done
about it in a given period of time, what it will cost the company in sales and profits, and what effect it might have on
the company's employees and on the community.

It should be clear to every spokesman for the firm that
scare tactics have little value. To declare that the plant will
have to close if the company is forced to correct a bad condition will carry weight only in the rare case where the community is captive to the company. Moreover, even in such situations the public has shown a remarkable obstinacy.
Extreme statements are more likely to win the moderates in
the community over to the viewpoint of the company's oppo-
nents. In addition, the company that threatens closing of its
plant probably has made the same threat in the past and
failed to carry through—perhaps on the occasion of a unionization drive, a strike for wages or benefits, or the penetration
of the labor market by another employer. Threats that failed
to materialize will be remembered by the public.

Another pitfall for managers is the temptation to use a report about environmental damage as a means to cover up errors of their own. Frequently it is convenient to ride the tail
of an emergency in order to obscure past mistakes. But the
danger is that this sort of intellectual dishonesty will be un-

covered, not by the board of directors but by the company's critics, who will then question the corporation's integrity. This might decisively end the manager's career.

Nor should the company misrepresent the financial outlay involved in the correction of an unfavorable condition. To combine the cost of such a project with a capital expansion program and announce the total figure as the cost of improving the environment will only lead to distrust of the corporation. Not only will the community react unfavorably, but through the news media the misrepresentation might be made a nationwide issue.

When a condition is found that is detrimental to the environment, the company should report it as accurately and comprehensively as possible. If speed is essential to prevent sensation-seeking outsiders from breaking the story, a preliminary report can be issued. Obviously no manager should take it upon himself to make a public announcement that involves the corporate image; close cooperation between top management and the board of directors is necessary. Management's obligation is to inform the directors, who as representatives of the stockholders will decide the course to follow.

But suppose that the manager finds himself in the position of advocating a plan that the board of directors or stockholders refuse to support. It may be that they are correct from a strictly financial point of view. Or it may be that different conclusions can be drawn from the same body of facts. Whatever the reason, differences of opinion will develop. What must the manager do when this happens?

First he must make every effort to see all facets of the problem. It is easy for an originator to become emotionally involved with his own creation and to overlook the alternatives that exist. Second, he must analyze the directors' refusal objectively. Did it result from a misunderstanding? Can it be reversed by a more carefully drawn up exposition? Were the manager's recommendations rejected only as a short-term expedient that will soon be past? If any of these reasons ac-

count for the board's refusal, the astute manager will reevaluate his position. Humility may be one of the rarest virtues
found in dynamic managers; still, it should have its place.

But what if analysis indicates that the difference of opinion between the manager and the board cannot be resolved?
The manager then has three alternatives.

The first is to accept the decision and, ignoring his own
beliefs, yield to the higher authority. By doing so, however,
he may destroy his effectiveness both to the company and to
himself. With respect to the company, he may well feel that
his future recommendations will not be viewed objectively—
that because he accepted a decision which was violently op-
posed to his convictions, he will be seen as a man of expediency. With respect to himself, he may feel that he no longer
has the strength of character to stand for what he believes to
be right.

The second alternative is to accept the decision and attempt to change the board's view. However, this course has
at least three traps: (1) It may be considered a rationalization
for a personal defeat, and the manager may be no better off
than in the first case. (2) The manager may convince himself
that he is fighting the system from within, whereas in fact his
actions show that he has surrendered. (3) In attempting to
change conditions, he may aggravate a sensitive situation and
be fired because he can no longer work within the organization.

The third alternative is for the manager to carefully examine his position and that of his opposition. If he convinces
himself that he is correct and they are wrong, and if he feels
that to accept the decision would be to seriously compromise
his principles, he may have to quit his job. Obviously this is a
drastic step and should be taken only after he has discussed
his dilemma with his supervisors. The prospect of finding
oneself unemployed, and facing the loss of significant fringe
benefits as well as a salary, can be a strong deterrent. Still, it
is not inconceivable that a manager could become a better

executive and a better person as a result. His superiors, too, could be so impressed by his resignation that they might reexamine their position and conclude that they were wrong.

As the field of management rapidly expands to include problems and issues outside the interests of today's managers, the complexity of decision making and the challenges involved will increase at an even greater rate. It will take strong men and women to respond to these new demands.

The Profit-Safety Squeeze

In contrast to the many and sometimes obscure causes of environmental damage, the failure to build a safe product can usually be blamed on management alone. It is most unlikely that any group of owners would direct their managers to build products which were unsafe or dangerous. Many executives may feel they are forced to do this when given the mandate to produce a profit or else; still, the decision on how to make that profit rests with them.

In an effort to produce the lowest-cost item with the highest possible profit, a group of managers may conclude that the only option left them is to sacrifice good design for a less than safe product. The folly of this decision is too well established to expound. A large company that produces a dangerous or even potentially unsafe item may be able to withstand the bad publicity and financial loss resulting from discontinuance of the product. A smaller organization may never recover. The manager caught in the squeeze between a safety requirement and a profit demand has only one course of action: He must design safety into the product, then work to find other ways of lowering the cost. The lure of cheap design is a trap for the naïve.

The world reputation for shoddy goods used to belong to the Japanese, but they have learned that much larger profits can be made from quality products. It would be a sad twist of fate if American industry picked up that discarded badge of dishonor and took over the Japanese junk business. Unfortunately, too many inferior products are being produced in this country. Most often, the excuse of competition is given to justify the action. More likely, the reason is poor and sloppy design condoned by an inept management. Both stockholders and the public deserve better from business managers. And fellow managers have a right to expect higher standards of performance from their peers.

Advertising: The Old Shell Game

A company which allows its product to be promoted with claims that are false, misleading, or purposely vague is in effect acknowledging the inadequacy of what it wants the public to purchase. It is in the same league with the sharpies who sold Dr. Quack's miracle elixers, since what both are doing is overwhelming the buyer with visual and verbal sleight-of-hand tricks—pulling a fast one on the rube with money in his wallet.

Yet today sharp practice in advertising seems pervasive in American business. Misleading claims by manufacturers are, with only minor differences, duplicated by banks, lending agencies, brokerage houses, theater producers, television networks, and just about every segment of business that competes for the consumer's dollar. Is there any difference between the cigarette manufacturer who slyly suggests that smoking his brand of cigarettes is as exhilarating as riding the range, and the finance company that advertises a rate of interest one-third the true annual charge? Or how about the drug manufacturer who suggests to the desperately ill that his product will bring relief (though it will not) and perhaps even a cure (though it will not)? Or the brokerage house that allows its customer men to promote a stock for which it is an agent without revealing this relationship? Or banks which give the impression that loans are available to everyone, without advertising that borrowers must have a certain credit rating? Or the television station that "stages" news items for the benefit of a gullible public? Or theater producers who take excerpts from unfavorable reviews and use them out of context to promote their plays?

Indeed, considering the abuses of confidence that the buying public must contend with, it is miraculous that angry people have not insisted on more reform and control than they are now demanding. When the housewife struggles to determine price per unit weight of foods that are similar but not identical, or attempts to evaluate grades of products with shades of differences, or wonders whether her eyes are giving out when she sees a large box selling at a higher cost per pound than a smaller one, she is being treated to the old shell game. The same game challenges the motorist who is trying to decide on the safest and best tire for his money. And the trap is no different for businessmen interested in buying another company who are struggling with a CPA's report on assets and liabilities, or for the investor who is advised to buy a stock even while the officials of that company are quietly disposing of their holdings—strictly within the law.

It would not be difficult to conclude that most business is hypocrisy and deceit, that the rule "buyer beware" prevails, and that every consumer must pit his wits against unscrupulous sellers. There is much that is wrong and unhealthy in today's business climate, and a crisis seems to be developing between American sellers and buyers. The irony is that there is no need for it.

Collectively, the goods and services offered for sale in America today are better than any in the world. That there are higher-quality foreign-made items in specific categories of the selling spectrum does not negate this contention. Production in America was developed to make available to the mass of buyers a relatively reliable and inexpensive choice of goods, and it has succeeded admirably.

Dollar for dollar and pound for pound, American automobiles are the most inexpensive and reliable anywhere. Their design was conceived to satisfy middle-class owners, and it has done this remarkably well. Unquestionably there are some better lower- and higher-priced foreign imports, and the low-cost foreign car may capture an even larger percentage of the American market than it has to date. These automobiles are being offered to a specialty buyer and are satisfying a particular want. In no case, however, does this foreign competition justify American producers in exaggerating claims for their own cars.

No matter what the American manufacturers say, the safety features provided are not adequate to protect drivers in accidents resulting from the high speed built into the vehicle. Nor is safety the consumer's duty; there are simply too many variables, such as weather, road conditions, and road markings, to hold the driver responsible for knowing what type of automobile he can drive. The producer must take into account these and other factors—fatigue, reactions due to alcohol, the effect of the high concentration of pollutants on congested roadways, and the nonuniformity of driving conditions throughout the country—in designing, manufacturing, and promoting cars. Moreover, there is no justification for portraying any automobile as anything but a convenient, economical, comfortable, and frequently pleasant way of getting from one place to another. To suggest that it is a means of expressing personal frustrations by putting four hundred horses in competition with someone else's chariot is to boost the grim statistics of highway deaths.

As for the food industry, it is obvious that telling the housewife how many ounces of contents are in a can of fruit does not tell her all she needs to know about it. Nor does the government-imposed grade tell her whether the can contains half water and half fruit, or all fruit with a little water to keep it moist.

Certainly the food industry as a whole has made available

to consumers a wide selection of nutritious and inexpensive foods. Usually each was developed and packaged with a certain market in mind, and there is no reason why that market should not be served. But no consumers in any market should be subjected to buying conditions that preclude the possibility of an intelligent decision. The housewife with a child or two tugging at her skirts who is looking at a package of food and trying to decipher information that confuses experts is being taken in by sharp operators. Either they lack confidence in what they are selling, or they are producing an item that is not wanted and are trying to pretend that it is another product altogether.

The investor who attempts to wade through pages of footnotes to a yearly report; the home buyer who is confronted with points at a house closing; the borrower struggling to keep up payments that include usurious interest charges; company executives attempting to determine the true value of a prospective acquisition; theatergoers who spend a small fortune to sit through a play that was promoted by gimmickry; an industrial buyer waiting in vain for a delivery that has been promised repeatedly—these are all victims of the deceitful public relations in American business today. It is time that managers reached maturity. Deviousness is an expedient of people who are uncertain of themselves. American managers are the best anywhere, and they have inherited businesses from other managers who were the best in their time. Industry and its products have proved themselves; there is no need to continue using false sales pitches to sell goods.

The responses of American business to the ecological problem, to the issue of product safety, and to the question of truth in advertising all have a missing ingredient: integrity. This ingredient must become a part of the complex formula that makes up business life if managers expect to operate in a climate like the one in which their businesses developed— that is, in a relatively free and open marketplace.

Imagination in Social Action

An approach to the problems confronting managers, in this period of managerial confrontation with so many people who find so much wrong in management's way of doing business, will be found through imagination and initiative. It will take imagination of a high order to devise solutions for the multitude of particulars that must be put right. And it will require great initiative to launch the programs that change established business patterns.

Since the manager's resources are always limited, naturally he must channel them according to a system of priorities. First among these, no matter what the social reformers say, is the responsibility to produce profits. This will be true as long as ours is a relatively free economy. But to keep it free, businessmen must stop relying upon the government to make reforms that they do not find it convenient to initiate. In the short run it may be easier for an industry to wait for local, state, or national legislatures to require the installation of safety devices, investment in sewage- or smoke-purifying equipment, or more expensive designs to meet a new standard. Likewise, there may be short-term benefits in protective tariffs, government specification of advertising norms, and the imposition of grades and classes of products. What is inherent in each of these government-initiated actions, however, is loss of that much more freedom.

Nothing produces greater despair in those who truly believe in the free enterprise system than to observe that many proponents of this concept prefer socialistic practices wherever their own interests are involved. This is not to say that some cooperation and even concerted action are not desirable between industry and government. But it is to suggest that the road to government takeover of industry will be hastened if business leaders use the legislatures to effect changes that might meet opposition from the owners of the companies they manage.

The elimination of industrial damage to the environment, of unsafe products, and of routine dishonesty in advertising and promotion must originate with business. To take the initiative away from bureaucrats who now see themselves as the saviors of the buying public will require imagination of the caliber that produced some of the more exotic technical concepts managers have developed. It may be even more difficult, since social responsibility is outside their present areas of competence.

In running a plant, advertising a product, designing a machine, or offering a service, managers must recognize the faults of their operations and detail these conditions to the stockholders. They must show that certain problems demand special approaches, and they must learn how to secure cooperation from the government and understanding from the public in solving them.

As an example of what not to do, consider the unrealistic approach taken by the automobile manufacturers toward the solution of the exhaust problem. Each company is engaged in spirited competition with the others to develop a new type of unit that will most effectively reduce pollutants. Yet this is a perfect example of a problem on which industry can and should be pooling its resources. The imaginative approach that would benefit both the industry and the smog-choked public would be to develop a formula whereby information would be collected and initiative stimulated by awarding a bonus and a greater percentage of the profits to the developer of the most practical unit.

The same approach could be used by the industry to solve some of its other problems, such as that of producing a safer car. And the industry's entire resources could be mustered to find ways of eliminating the blight of automobile junkyards across the country. A jointly sponsored research team could devise the best ways of salvaging valuable parts from abandoned cars. Means for picking up the rest of the metal, compacting it, and delivering it to collection points could be developed. The work could be done through independent businesses or through company-sponsored organizations, and the manufacturer of an abandoned car would be assessed an amount covering the cost of the operation. The charge would be passed on to the consumer when he bought a car as his contribution to a cleaner environment.

This discussion has put the spotlight on automobile manufacturers because the number of people involved in the manufacture, sales, and service of cars makes the industry the largest single employer in the nation. It also turns out the product that creates the greatest pollution problem and the largest amount of litter. Other industries that degrade the environment are the metal, glass, paper, and plastic container producers, electric utility companies, metal and paper processing industries, gas and oil refineries, rubber and cement processors, the airlines, and the thousands of small and medium-size companies that line the country's rivers and streams. It is imperative that they show imagination in finding ways —perhaps unorthodox as measured by past company practices—to eliminate or significantly reduce problems of the environment.

Their approaches may take the form of joint ventures, association-sponsored research and production facilities, or white papers that outline an industry condition, appraise the situation, and make proposals for eliminating the problem on a detailed timetable. They may conduct studies of ways to attack a problem through cooperative efforts by industry, government, and the public. Or they may simply make it company policy to be "clean" from plant to product to disposal of the used product.

In the combined drive by industry, government, and the public that must emerge, industry should not be a follower but a leader. It is up to managers, as guardians of our industrial wealth and as citizens affected by the use made of their output, to exert a major influence on the decisions that will change what they are doing.

Managers should develop programs that will eliminate undesirable side effects from the facilities and products. They should be able to show that the causes are attributable to the public and the government as well as to the company. They should promote compromise plans whereby the company receives tax benefits for making an investment to correct a problem that adversely affects ecology. Municipalities could be persuaded to suspend taxes for a certain number of years on an addition to a facility which eliminates an undesirable condition. State and federal governments could be convinced that legislation is needed to provide tax relief, either through faster write-offs or reduced capitalization, or through income tax reductions, where money is spent on improving facilities to correct a bad situation. Low-interest loans, guaranteed by the government, might be made to small or needy companies. Certainly laws should not be punitive, except to apply sanctions against companies that refuse to correct a condition after the means have been made available.

Competing companies could join forces in establishing junk pickup stations throughout the country, financed by nontaxable grants made on an assessed basis according to percentage of the company's product found in the junk. To assume that individual companies, working by themselves, can clean up centuries of accumulated industrial filth is unrealistic. It is equally fallacious to conclude that industry alone can do the job; industrial leadership must be supported by the public, as the biggest single contributor to the ugliness of our countryside, and government, as a partner in what is derived from industrial activity. No one will gain if a company is forced out of business because it could not correct a faulty plant or product and still compete in the marketplace.

If any reminder is needed as to the extent of the problem and the danger of continued fouling of the air, land, and water, one need only visit any large city anywhere in the country on a smoggy day. Or look at the rivers flowing through and around the cities, or the filth littering the countryside. The problem is pressing, and it will be solved only by a task force effort. In this effort it is up to managers to see that a cleaner environment is not won through lost freedom.

Management Takes the Initiative

Besides the imagination that will be required to create new programs for today's problems in industry, managers will need strength and determination to formulate and implement these programs. A manager may find it necessary to indict himself in explaining an unfavorable condition: a decision that he made in the past may now come back to haunt him. Or his investigation of a problem may disclose poor judgment on the part of his colleagues or predecessors. Fault-finding at such close quarters may take more intestinal fortitude than most managers have. Yet the recognition of the problem and the reasons for its existence will go a long way toward preventing its repetition in the future.

This is not to say that any manager is expected to be a martyr; a manager's first objective is to continue to manage. Up to the present he achieved that objective by being a good profit producer; from now on he will also be required to show that profits will continue in the future—that they will not be jeopardized by the need to spend large sums to correct something that should have been corrected before. A manager is measured not by one wrong decision but by the total of the decisions he makes over a period of time, including those that may contribute to his successor's performance record rather than his own. Sometimes he will find it necessary to acknowledge his own bad judgment, learn from it, and make sure that his future decisions avoid the same error.

In correcting some conditions, it may be necessary for a manager to program for a lower present profit and convince the owners that this course will pay off in increased future earnings. Such an action, which is contrary to everything the manager has trained himself to do, takes great determination and confidence. But it is the sort of imaginative thinking and initiative that will enable managers to retain the power of self-determination—to decide for themselves where their industries will be going in the future.

There must be a return to integrity by managers in the utilization of the resources entrusted to them. They must sell their product, not what some sharp marketeer thinks is their product. They must not sacrifice safety or reliability in an effort to turn a quick profit. Managers are typical Americans in that they are members of this society and unique in that they have been given stewardship of what is produced and sold. To the extent that they deceive their customers, they in turn are being deceived, because the world they are making is one that they and their own offspring will not enjoy.

The manager must be willing to create outside his previous area of creativity and to extend his initiative outside his historic field of endeavor. Unless he does so, he may find that others are formulating the ideas by which he must live and that his vaunted drive and energy are expended in fighting to break the shackles that enmesh him.

3

A Wasteland
of Unused Manpower

W<small>HILE</small> the manager has been occupied with popular indignation over his waste of nature's material resources and his pollution of the environment, a less publicized but potentially greater conflict is developing over his inability to make good use of large segments of the population. Young men, men in late middle age, nonwhite men of all ages, and women as a group all form a vast wasteland of unused and unwanted manpower that will become an increasingly severe problem. This chapter will treat the various groups of men; Chapter 4 will examine the predicament of women in American business.

Some Statistics

In a results-oriented economy, there is no room for the low producer. An employee either meets a standard or is replaced by someone who can; nothing could be fairer than this.

Or could it? While such reasoning may be equitable in terms of logic, it may be most unjust in terms of life. It is often cruel to those who must play the game without having the opportunity to improve their performance.

The results of a business policy that demands skilled workers without providing the means for people to develop these skills can be seen from statistics on young men entering the workforce. This country is increasing its working population by approximately 2,627,000 young men each year. Of those between the ages of sixteen and twenty-one, 1,650,000 were high school graduates not headed for college, and 977,-000 were school dropouts.[1] Furthermore, during a period when the annual rate of unemployment was estimated at 3.1 percent for all males sixteen years and over,[2] the rate for whites in the sixteen to twenty-one group was 7.6 percent, while a startling 11.8 percent of the nonwhites were out of work.[3]

At the other end of the scale, it is estimated that the number of men between the ages of fifty-five and sixty-five will increase from 8,942,000 in 1968 to 9,745,000 in 1980.[4] In this age group there will be a decline in the relative number in the labor force, since many will undoubtedly take advantage of changes in the Social Security Act and the improvement of private pension plans.[5]

A Short History of American Manpower

The strength of this nation came from the manpower that furnished the muscles and brains required to support its tre-

[1] U.S. Department of Labor, Bureau of Labor Statistics, *Monthly Labor Review* (August 1970), Table 2, p. 38.
[2] *Monthly Labor Review* (October 1969), Table 7, p. 99.
[3] *Monthly Labor Review* (August 1970), Table 3, p. 38.
[4] *Monthly Labor Review* (May 1970), Table 1, p. 4.
[5] Ibid., p. 11.

mendous growth. At times the young country was so short of help that it recruited men and their families from Europe and hired coolies from China. Even then the demand for labor was so great that women were employed in menial tasks and children of seven and eight worked as breaker boys and bobbin carriers and wipers in coal mines, textile works, and machine shops. Laborers and skilled workers put in ten- and twelve-hour days, and six-day weeks.

On occasion a recession or depression would occur, and the newly organized unions, supported by increasingly vocal social reformers, would seize the opportunity to demand reduced employment for women and children and shorter workdays and workweeks for everyone. These demands were slowly met, and managers had to find ways of compensating for the higher cost of labor. Their lower-paid employees were removed from the workforce, while the weekly wages of the other workers remained fixed or even rose for fewer hours of work.

Managers studied the jobs and developed better ways to do them, and the result was a larger output of lower-cost products that sold to wider markets. Unceasingly the means of production—labor, machinery, and facilities—were analyzed in detail. And as the hours of effort put forth by the man in the shop decreased, his pay increased.

In the Great Depression of the thirties, however, the country found itself with an overabundance of labor. The underlying reasons for this failure of the system never were deciphered, nor were means found to reverse what happened. While Keynesian economic measures were being instituted, a force of major dimensions was shaping up in Europe: Hitler was consolidating his power.

The American industrial complex began to tool up to produce for the Allied nations and the surplus of manpower evaporated. With Pearl Harbor came a grave shortage of men as both soldiers and producers. The retired toolmaker, the displaced farmer, the high school dropout too young to fight, and the migrating black were accepted for jobs without concern about anything but their willingness to work, at least occasionally. Even then, demand outran supply. Rosie the Riveter came to the shop, and others like her joined the armed services.

Despite the shortage of labor, runaway inflation was avoided during and immediately after the war through wage and price controls, curtailed consumer production, and a tightly controlled economy. But economists, government planners, and businessmen feared that the postwar economy might simply revert to its prewar Depression level. They overlooked the backlog of consumer needs and wants that had built up over years of wartime privation. And they did not foresee the demand for a better life by the well-paid war workers, or the determination of the veteran to improve his lot after having been exposed to higher standards in the armed forces.

A second period of expansion burst upon a surprised but pleased country. Then before the economy was even fully geared to meet the demands of domestic buyers, the Cold War took on aspects of a hot encounter. The country found itself on the battlefield less than ten years after the war to end wars had been won. The economy supported a heavy consumer demand and a demand for military goods to fight a war in the mountains of Korea.

Thus began twenty years of unequaled industrial expansion. It was a time during which the country ventured abroad as explorer, policeman, and combatant; accepted the Russian challenge to a space race; and tried to satisfy the wants of an increasingly affluent and materially oriented population. The success of these efforts was not total. The foreign ventures led to increasing frustration with the standoff in Korea, the psychological defeat in Cuba, and the inability to win decisively or lose gracefully in Vietnam. Weary of the Asian adventure, the populace indicated its wish for an honorable but measured withdrawal from the rice paddies of Indochina. There was a perceptible reduction in military spending which in itself was not too difficult for the economy to take.

The space race with Russia came to a climax as Neil Armstrong took his giant step for mankind on the moon. Instead of being stimulated by victory, however, the nation seemed willing to wait and reflect before embarking on manned voyages beyond the moon. Reacting to this mood, the government made still another reduction in spending as it postponed new space adventures. Again, the economy could have absorbed this shock if it had happened alone.

The economy had produced more goods and satisfied more wants than ever before, but it had grown flabby in filling military, space, and domestic needs. The practice to acquire unneeded plants and people in anticipation of even greater demand, without worrying too much about when or how they would be paid for, became widespread. A speculative fever infected large numbers of people who had watched the curve of prosperity climb monotonously upward. In the same period the demand for workers and supervisory personnel had stimulated hard-pressed managers to find ways to get more output from the limited number of employees they had available.

The first year of the 1970s came in with the barometer of business, the stock market, giving readings of grave misapprehension about the stability of the economy. Many forecasters assumed that, after a rather heady and frequently reckless frolic, the bull was simply resting for another romp. After a few months, however, it became clear that the economy was doing more than resting. Something was basically wrong with it. The cutbacks in military budgets (harmless in themselves), coupled with the reduced space exploration expenditures (not too significant alone), combined with the decision to halt an accelerating inflation (commendable and necessary for the long-range well-being of the economy), resulted in a severe blow to American business. In an effort to retain profits managers reacted in characteristic fashion, cutting costs, curtailing expenditures, shelving expansion plans—and reviewing personnel with a sharp eye.

Employees in the higher age brackets who were too old to adapt to tighter standards were eased into early retirement or terminated as unfit.

The army of workers, both black and white, who had been recruited from the ranks of the underprivileged and unskilled were terminated, while seniority protected those who were more entrenched. School dropouts and even high school graduates had nothing to offer the suddenly persnickety employer. They were not only uneducated by today's standards but unemployable according to the newly developed job requirements.

Thus the nation found itself with a labor force of unwanted skilled but elderly men, undereducated black and white youths, and unskilled black and white underprivileged of all ages. A vast wasteland of unused and unwanted men and women existed in a country busy satisfying its needs without them. Moreover, as the economy prepares to become profitably efficient against growing competition from within and without, this group of lost people will increase, unless something is done to convert it from a restless mass into a contributing group of builders and buyers. Here is a challenge that must be explored today so that management can meet it tomorrow.

Old Is Out

What is an "old" employee?

What causes a manager to conclude that one of his men, supervisor or supervised, has reached an age where he is no longer productive? Why should a man at a given age be considered too old for a given position? If the answers to these questions were clear and universal in application, the problem of the so-called old employee would be easier to solve.

There are few well-accepted criteria for determining whether or not a man is too old to do a particular job. The most obvious is that of physical ability. To take an extreme example, few professional football teams would be interested in taking on a forty-year-old quarterback. And if football strategy were somehow changed so that it required the agility, reflexes, and endurance of men in the twenty- to twenty-five-year range, the problem of unemployed quarterbacks would become considerably larger. This is what frequently happens in the world of business and industry.

Whenever a new process or method is developed numbers of men are unable to cope with the mental or physical demands required to perform satisfactorily. They are no longer needed. In the case of the lone quarterback, someone may see value in his experience and employ him as a trainer or coach. Likewise, the exceptional man in business or industry who finds his job made obsolete often gets another job where his knowledge can be used. But it is doubtful whether more than an occasional talented man is absorbed in this fashion. The lot of those replaced by newer and better means of production is usually unemployment.

This happens to talented managers who, in a reorganization or an acquisition, find themselves competing with younger but equally skilled men for newly created positions. Higher management, weighing more years of service against a potential that covers a greater working span, will opt for the younger men.

In a recession or a period of great competition, cost-cutting studies focus on salaries, and the older employee is frequently on the higher end of the wage scale. Probably a younger understudy can do the work fairly well, with more vigor and application, and for a much lower salary.

Some men find themselves physiologically or mentally old while they are still relatively young in years. They become incapable of doing the work they should, even though they have performed well for years. Most companies, not accustomed to reassigning men within the organization because of the "bad effects" on others, find ways to ease such men out.

In contrast to the prematurely aged employee is the one who finds himself forced to retire on a given birthday, even though he is mentally alert and physically capable of handling the job.

These groups of men find that after years of service to a company, they are old and no longer wanted. There was a time when men of sixty-five were considered the backbone of their companies; it was they who had the know-how to run the operation. But as the trend toward mechanization of procedures, standards, and organization took on more "scientific" aspects, the dependence on human knowledge was minimized, and impersonal means of retaining and utilizing data took precedence.

Men were no longer required to have a great store of knowledge. On the contrary, too much information on a given subject could make it difficult to unlearn old rules and learn new ones. A man's knowledge might make him inflexible, so that the company could suffer from his occupational senility. The employee in demand was the one who could adapt to changing circumstances, fads, and innovations. He was not so encrusted with tradition and methodology that he could not see the potential good in the most extreme approach to a problem. Experience in other companies gave him a broad background, and from it he could envision a variety of ways of doing things. Since men as they grow older tend to take comfort in worn and time-tested habits, it was obvious that only younger men could have the psychological plasticity to react to the needs of the developing managerial style.

Old was out; young was in.

However, since no one has been able to define "old" satisfactorily, its interpretation invariably falls to the person who is concerned with applying his brand of new management. Today the label "old" seems to descend on middle managers between the ages of forty-five and fifty, depending upon the industry and the job. Once a man has reached the golden age of fifty in most fields, his chances of acquiring a job leading to higher potential diminish rapidly. But there are areas in the business environment where forty-five is a dangerous age for unemployment, as in the fast-moving fields of computer utilization and design.

Yet in reality, there is no reason for declaring a man too old for any job except where physical agility is a prerequisite. The simple act of operating a machine may require certain physical and mental responses that some men do not possess. While it may be that a greater number of older men are less able to qualify for such jobs, it is equally certain that there are men of *all* ages who cannot do them. The point is to determine who can and who cannot. Furthermore, where it is a man on the managerial level who is discriminated against because of age, the company may be discarding him at a time when its younger managers are in dire need of his knowledge and independence of judgment..

Besides the current fad for youth, there are other reasons why older employees are not wanted in many companies:

Often when a younger manager takes over, he convinces himself that the older executives have become so set in their ways that constructive change is impossible. Sometimes he is right, but usually analysis will show that what these executives are following is the policy of an acknowledged leader of the organization (who is not necessarily the top man). If this leader is relieved of his duties, and new thinking is introduced at his level, the other managers' accumulated knowledge can be an asset to the entire operation.

Sometimes, on the other hand, there is a clean sweep of all men classified as old; new drivers are brought in and, charged and charging, destroy the organization before they come to understand its workings.

In other situations older men are let go because they are astute enough to see that a proposed course of action will result in disaster, and out of loyalty to the company they will not remain silent.

Or they are cased out because they do not show enough

enthusiasm for a change that will make the company vulnerable if the innovation does not succeed. Their experience cautions them against burning their bridges.

Sometimes older men are considered a liability when a company decides to change its image from that of a conservatively managed one to that of an aggressive, results-oriented producer.

Or company planners may conclude that a reorganized managerial team must be put together with men who will grow with the organization over the next ten or fifteen years. The man who is fifty-five or sixty does not qualify for the new team.

Employees with long tenure may know too much—such as where the bodies are buried. It is much safer and more relaxing to have simon-pure men in the managerial structure.

A manager likes to be surrounded by people who reflect his thinking and his way of operating, and those who see eye to eye with him are usually close to his own age.

Reasoning that produces conclusions such as these is misguided. To act on the basis of age in replacing men is to draw upon generalizations that are sometimes correct and sometimes incorrect. There are other generalizations that can be made in favor of older men:

The older employee is very often a loyal man—a virtue not to be overlooked in this age of uncertain loyalties.

The continuity that the older employee gives a company may be the ingredient holding together an operation that is unstable for other reasons. His accrued knowledge may be the only repository for key pieces of information.

The man who has learned to work with and supervise other employees is a valuable asset; one does not readily find good top supervisors. If he leaves, competent young people who were working under him may leave too.

A company can derive much benefit from utilizing older employees as consultants. The older machine operator or craftsman can implement training or apprentice programs for industrial jobs that today are going unfilled because firms have not shown sufficient initiative in developing such projects. Managers, too, can be used as consultants in areas where their knowledge and independence will balance the ambitions and speculative schemes of younger men. In addition, the development and experimentation that many big companies badly need in the field of managerial organization can be conducted by a cadre of older managers who know the company's goals and needs and who are free of daily operational pressures.

A final consideration might be the value in morale to the entire organization when older employees are used productively. Instead of reluctantly advancing toward that inevitable birthday, employees know that they are merely moving from one stage to another which is different but is not closed off from everything they have been familiar with.

This is not to suggest that it is not wise and frequently necessary to replace men because of age. Nor is it to say that an age limit which makes retirement mandatory should not exist in a company. What is proposed is that many men at all ages are capable of valuable contributions to the nation's economy, and that they can probably work better if they stay in their own companies than if they are forced to move. In the future, the number of men in the upper age brackets will increase, and the problem of what to do with them should not be evaded by deciding to fire or retire them. The real question is how this wealth of information and talent can be utilized. To let it go by default is an extravagance that this country cannot afford.

The Underprivileged and the Nonwhite

Underprivileged and unskilled men, white and nonwhite, have learned that their talents are not much in demand, particularly when the economy is working at less than maximum capacity. This is a country that rewards the individual who "creates" his own opportunities and penalizes the one who has not been astute enough to share in the national largess. It is a country that is too busy to take time to train its help but would rather operate through a method of switch-and-try in selecting employees as they are needed. Consequently millions of men are ill-prepared for any work but the most menial and unskilled, and the number of people in this group will continue to grow as companies work to reduce production costs.

The fact is that today most hand operations could probably be eliminated from high-volume production. The technology exists to automate any physical movement as well as many semi-intelligent activities. In producing its new low-cost automobile, General Motors announced in 1970 that spot welding of the chassis would be 90 percent machine-performed, as compared with 20 percent on other cars. The sophistication of automated processes is shown in the complex operation of analyzing blood samples, which originally required skilled laboratory technicians but has been performed by machinery for some years.

Technological advances are well ahead of the ability of industry and society to absorb them without major disruptions. In agriculture, when scientific farming made it possible to produce more than could be sold, farmers were paid to put acreage into "banks"; they were paid not to produce. Industry too is reaching a point where men are being placed in banks and paid not to produce. Their pay is in the form of unemployment and welfare stipends. When demand for labor goes up, they are withdrawn from the bank and put to work, only to be sent back to inventory when demand falls again.

A rising chorus is protesting against the practice of treating human beings as nothing more than one of the factors in the economic formula. When we think of production as the process of applying labor to materials to create a good, it is easy to forget that the factor of labor consists of humans. Of the various items in the production formula, humanity is the only natural resource that can resupply itself; all others are depleted and lost. This fact has enabled technologists to rationalize a lack of concern for the unemployed, since there will always be an ample supply of people to fill the needs of industry.

On balance, American businesses have failed as employers. While performing brilliantly as innovators of new products and ideas and as producers and distributors of goods, they have relegated the job of caring for their employees to others. Two agencies alien to the business world have attempted to fill the void: the government and the labor unions have taken up the role of defenders of the workingman. As would be expected, they are doing a very poor job. Since theirs is a defensive role, they do not correct a bad situation but merely try to alleviate it. The simple fact is that employers are the ones who create, bestow, and preserve jobs. It is only through business and industry that the problem of finding employment for the underprivileged and for minority groups can be solved. Unless tomorrow's manager wants to wait for governmental action or for coercion from a union, he will begin immediately to work on this problem.

People should be hired with the objective of upgrading them on a routine basis. This will require a reversal in the approach of many planning and work-study people, who see their task as the simplification of jobs. In many industries, particularly those with assembly line operations, companies are finding it difficult even in hard-core poverty areas to find employees who are willing to do the boring and depressing jobs they are assigned. Of course, the introduction of more complex and more interesting ways of working will lead to higher labor costs. Or will it? The drop in labor turnover and the reduction in absenteeism resulting from more satisfying work could in the end reduce costs. And the greater buying power of the new employees might expand the market for products to bring in a greater overall profit.

Another step that could be taken is to make jobs available to the underprivileged at the place where they live or else to provide them with transportation to the job. Certainly the company that undertakes to transport employees from a depressed neighborhood, or to build a plant in some remote area to provide work for the underprivileged, should be given tax relief to offset the added costs and lowered profitability. Today there are small programs of these kinds, as well as one that favors bidders from depressed areas on government contracts. And in almost every instance, this pilot work is being sponsored by some government agency.

Above all, consideration must be given to nonwhites as employees. No amount of rationalization can excuse the fact that they have been prejudged because of their color. Mexican Americans, Puerto Ricans, and Indians have not received the publicity that the blacks have, but all have been judged equally harshly on the basis of the pigment in their skin. In the past whenever speech or dress were the distinguishing features of a minority group, a person could become assimilated by the simple expedient of learning passable English or buying a new suit. The nonwhite has no such escape; his color is fast.

The accumulated prejudices and assumptions about the capabilities of nonwhite Americans must be overcome. It will not be easy, since a counterreaction has developed in these people who have been denied for so long. Suppressed needs and desires are surfacing in violent outbursts as nonwhites recognize that meek acquiescence produces nothing, while aggressiveness brings results. Managers cannot afford to judge men on the basis of color any more than they were ever justified in evaluating them according to the color of their school tie.

Ways must be found to make opportunities available for nonwhites. They must be elevated to jobs they are not prepared to handle, put into positions that have been created to help them advance, judged on their ability to adapt and learn from a different base than their white competitor, and welcomed into the circle of managers. If this approach carries a penalty in the form of somewhat lowered efficiency and productivity, it is the price that must be paid for years of neglect and callousness by yesterday's and today's managers.

What is suggested is that managers, independently of leadership from the government, undertake to prove that they mean it when they say their most valuable asset is their employees. It is obvious that most non-industry-initiated programs are almost certain to fail, if only because their sponsors do not have the necessary control over industry to make them succeed. At least, they do not have that control yet.

Because industry has regularly resisted improvements in the welfare of its employees, whether in unemployment benefits, safety, hours of work, equality in hiring practices, and a long list of other protective benefits it eventually accepted, the government through legislation has become much more industry's partner than is generally recognized. The time has come to stop such encroachment by bureaucracy. Government officials may be interested in doing good, but they do not recognize the bad results of their efforts. Industry must stop making itself the target for social agitators who are certain of their cause but could not care less about the long-term problems their solutions create. And the time to stop is before government, unions, and social activists have completely taken over the initiative and the response from industry is nothing but reaction to what is being proposed.

Business managers can take the initiative by being adventurous in their thinking and bold in their actions. Revising their favorite dogmas, they must look into new theories and propositions—for example, into the feasibility of tailoring jobs to employees rather than having people conform to job descriptions. They must weigh the benefits of a stable and satisfied group of employees against the costs of a disgruntled and unsettled workforce, and they must think in terms of retaining employees rather than of laying them off during times of economic stress.

If he is to retain his present operational freedom, the manager in tomorrow's world will set these and similar approaches high on the list of business priorities. Large groups of men and women, of all colors and races, are giving signs that they are unwilling to be numbered, disposable ingredients in the industrial process. The underprivileged are weary of the cyclical frustration of being "half-and-halfers"—half employed and half unemployed. There is still time to prevent a major incursion by the government, acting through legislation brought about by restless voters and vociferous pressure groups.

Dropouts and High School Graduates

Young is in.

That is the statement made earlier, and it is true, relatively speaking. Now, it must be qualified, for when we look at the really young people entering the labor market for the first time, quite a different picture emerges. During the recent recession the Labor Department reported that in October 1969, approximately 11.2 percent of males between the ages of sixteen and twenty-one were unemployed, while the figure was 23.2 percent for school dropouts between the ages of sixteen and seventeen.[6] If the trend toward a more automated type of production continues, it is probable that the number of these unemployed will increase more rapidly. And the automation trend is not confined to the production floor: Where young typists used to be hired to turn out form letters, the newer copying machines reproduce a page that is almost identical with the original. Or if actual typing is desired, a

[6] *Monthly Labor Review* (August 1970), Table 3, p. 38.

typewriter with a memory exists that will run off as many copies as ordered. The file clerk is being replaced by the computer, which stores and finds information far more accurately and swiftly than the fastest girl.

Training and apprentice programs have all but disappeared from the business scene. Unions have tightened their control over hiring practices so that except in rare cases, young men with technical school training cannot qualify for semiskilled jobs or trades. Approximately 50 percent of high school graduates are now going on to college. The other half, joining dropouts in the workforce, are having increasing difficulty finding jobs. Managers who think that this problem is not theirs might reflect that they are the visible authority which either accepts or rejects a job applicant, and as such they are the focus of attention.

What the riot and the rock festival reflect are the boredom and hopelessness of young people who have no objectives in life and no activity to give direction to the aimless path they are following. It would be wrong to say that adults are responsible for the individual acts of violence that the young commit, but what was or was not done by older people certainly did lead directly to the conditions that exist. Even in paradise, of course, there would be disgruntled and destructive young people. Yet what is happening among today's youth points to a failure of the adult world to anticipate and prepare for the needs of coming generations.

Managers must work toward reconciling the need to be producers of profit with the obligation to insure that what they are building will still be here in ten or twenty years. They must accept responsibility for assimilating large numbers of young people into the workforce, for making them into contributors to society, and for helping them become relatively satisfied members of a laboring community.

The practice of elevating the requirements of routine jobs to the level of college-trained applicants, though self-defeating, is widespread. The company that does this can boast about the extraordinarily large number of college graduates on its workforce, despite the fact that turnover is excessive as bored employees quit and are replaced with other college graduates.

Many jobs could be made available to the less well-educated and -trained young person if companies were willing to assume the task of training him for future utilization on their staff. Managers who need skilled men in their operations complain of the difficulty of finding replacements for retiring employees and of staffing expanding work centers. Yet the efforts of business are almost nonexistent in the area of job training and apprenticeship programs. Instead of concentrating on elevating the nonprofessional staff, management tends to take the attitude that factory workers are necessary but undesirable elements in business. The long-range objective has not been to find ways of retaining and expanding this group; rather, it has been to devise methods for keeping it as small as possible. The drive to increase the output per employee has meant nothing more than an effort to turn out the same amount of goods with fewer people, or to increase output with the same workforce. The manager must think of employees as long-term assets who can be brought in young, trained and retrained as needs for talents and skills change, and expanded as a group to create a stable society that is a consumer of products instead of a destroyer of the means of production.

Management and Manpower

The manager's problem is to use fewer hours of labor per unit of output, yet to employ more people—all the while showing an increasing profit. To accomplish these apparently divergent objectives he must develop ways to increase the productivity of the total workforce. This will require a far greater understanding than we now have of what motivates employees. Accounting practices, too, must be extended to calculate losses due to absenteeism, tardiness, boredom, and destruction of property, and to balance these against gains derived from a motivated, satisfied, and interested group of employees. The problem of developing methods for arriving at the dollar values and for making meaningful comparisons remains to challenge the future manager.

The investment in socially necessary projects that are costly to the company and have no immediate visible return must also be weighed against the cost of allowing large segments of society to remain disillusioned and resentful of a system that seems designed to keep them from bettering themselves.

Manpower must be treated as something separate from the classical definition it has been given. Nothing could be more detrimental to a reasonable approach to solving the problem of unemployment than the practice of viewing men as a commodity in the production cycle.

Management must develop a more mature understanding of the part that industry plays in the life of the nation. American business is not merely the producer and dispenser of goods, the steward of owners who expect a reasonable return on their invested money. It is a dominant factor in the lives of every working (and potential working) person in the country. How business decides to treat these people determines how well or how poorly they live.

Industry's plans for the utilization of older people, the underprivileged, minority groups, and unskilled young people will go a long way to decide whether the country will be the fine place to live that some envision, or the armed and charcoal-scarred wasteland that is predicted by so many who have been discarded by today's society.

If, in order to shape this country's future, managers must discard some of the cherished notions they learned in business and engineering schools, they should do so. It would be ill-advised to insist upon old ways of running their businesses if it means that, tomorrow or the next day, what they are so carefully building today will be destroyed by violence or by government intervention. The extinction of ideals is as final and damaging to a civilization as any mob action; to prevent this from happening is the single biggest challenge confronting the future manager.

4

Women
on Executive Row

AFTER a millennium, women are about to become the recognized equals of men. At least, they are if legislation, placards, demonstrations, sit-ins, and debates in the mass media have anything to do with it. One thing is certain: With magnificent rapidity, women are expanding their participation in occupations and activities that were formerly considered the domain of men.

For some time it seemed that the feminist movement had run its course. Women received the right to vote. Largely through their efforts, Prohibition was enacted. The typewriter brought them into the office, and the atmosphere of business was changed forever. No longer did women need to hide in order to smoke or drink; these pleasures were available to all. As the two-car family became commonplace, the automobile was converted into an extension of the kitchen. On television and radio, stage and screen, as war correspondents or best-selling authors, women were competing with men on equal terms. What more could women possibly want?

Over the last few years, American men have been finding out. Sometimes they approved in characteristic male fashion

—with much gallant attention. At other times they responded with less chivalry.

Women are determined to become totally emancipated. As they expose more and more of their bodies, men are pleased—and show it. But women are not stopping there; they are used to such attention, and what they are after is more complex than man's lecherous glances. They want a part of his world. They demand the right to become jockeys, brokers, baseball umpires, bankers, and managers. These demands will not be satisfied easily. What women expect is total equality with men in any endeavor where their femininity does not directly conflict with the expected performance. Thus while women might hesitate to seek jobs as baritones, they may well demand to play in men's golf tournaments if they can avoid the cut. In other words, women will participate in every activity where their physical attributes do not positively exclude them.

It is a naïve executive who does not know that in short order he will be confronted by females expecting to participate at all levels of management. While he may doubt that a woman can handle the job of superintending a foundry or machine shop, no logical argument will prove the point; it will take the test of trial and failure before women agree.

If the contention that women will be entering all phases of management is correct—and it seems to be—then it is important to understand some of the reasons why this is happening, how women are preparing for it, when management can expect it to come about, and what will be required to assimilate the intruders.

Facts of Life

Of the 80,733,000 persons in the civilian labor force in 1969,[1] 29,898,000 were women. Of the total women employed,

[1] U.S. Department of Labor, Bureau of Labor Statistics, *Monthly Labor Review* (June 1970), Chart 1, p. 96.

6,501,000 were single, 17,595,000 were married and living with their husbands, 4,197,000 were widowed or divorced, and 1,505,000 were married but not living with their husbands. This group of working women represented 41.6 percent of the female population. Approximately 20 percent of the working females were widowed, divorced, or not living with their husbands, so that they were essentially heads of households.[2] Nearly two out of every five American workers are women.[3] Certainly even at this time, women represent a significant segment of the business and industrial life of the nation.

The occupational history of women has gone from a period early in the development of business when they worked in the fields and factories shoulder to shoulder with men, through a time when it was considered enlightened to "protect" the female with restrictive legislation, to the present when it is contended that there is nothing, from umpiring a baseball game to managing a bank, that this sex cannot do. Men's bars have all but disappeared, and the girls are elbowing their way into the jockey's dressing room; women sell stocks and bonds, and they claim to be equal to men as chefs; the pretty revolutionary bomb thrower has supplanted the unshaved anarchist of years gone by. The woman of today has served notice that she wants access to every avenue and activity that she herself decides upon.

Indeed, if current legislation goes into effect, women will have the dubious honors of being eligible for the military draft, of being able to demand jobs in the coal mines, and of being required to pay alimony to their less fortunate divorced husbands. The simple fact is that today women are already involved in almost every activity men are; it is only a question of degree. There is no doubt that their participation will increase exponentially as the months and years advance. This greater involvement has significance for the future manager, because companies will soon be required to explain to some

[2] Ibid., Table 1, p. 13.
[3] Ibid., p. 2.

government agency why they have so few women as managers, assistants and assistant-to's, vice-presidents, and presidents.

Some commentators classify the current insistence on women's employment opportunities and civil and social rights as only another wave in the storm of dissatisfaction sweeping the nation. Others view it as a cyclically recurring phenomenon in which women demand some right or other that, in retrospect, all agree they should have had long ago. But today there is a new ingredient. In the past women could not escape from a simple fact of life: The means of birth control were at best unreliable, and despite excellent intentions, women who had decided upon a career might be forced to take maternity leave just as they began moving upward.

For better or worse, things have changed. The decision as to whether a woman will have a child or not is strictly hers. If she does become pregnant, she is free to take advantage of an abortion clinic, with expenses paid by her insurance plan. Reliable birth control devices and abortions are available in some states to single as well as married women in our newly enlightened society.

Marriage and the Family

With the acceptance of the idea that women are primarily responsible for determining conception and birth, the whole structure of family life has been placed in a new light. If the cornerstone of society is the family, then our entire social order may be weakening as well. Perhaps what is seen today in the uninhibited lives of some groups in our society is the sign of this trend. Future historians may conclude that the decline of modern civilization began with the emancipation of the female. However, if women continue to show the same understanding and patience in their relations with their opposites that they have exhibited up to this point, the outcome may be quite different. The history books may say that the renaissance of the twentieth century, emerging after a period of stagnant and boring modernism, began when women won equal responsibility in determining the course of events. One thing is certain: If the women of America suddenly took control of business and government, they could not create greater confusion than the men have already.

What will probably take place in the relationship between the sexes is that they will develop a hieghtened respect for one another as women begin to assume positions of equality with men in business, education, the professions, and civil affairs. Men may be pleasantly surprised to find that women are far more than helpless creatures in need of male assistance. Women's ingenuity, drive, ambition, dedication, intelligence—the total spectrum of qualities that the male has admired in them—may be seen in a new light as women display these strengths in career activities. Although men knew that women are capable of bravery and strength in trying home and family situations, somehow they did not recognize that the same traits could be expressed outside the home.

The woman of the future will have an enormous influence on the man in her life. In or out of wedlock, she will decide whether the family he wants coincides with her plans. Woman now can both actively pursue a career and function as a female—as she alone understands her role—without fear that she must forgo the former because of the latter. There will remain strong emotional and social pressures to raise a family within the socially accepted bonds of matrimony. Still, as the drive toward population control gains impetus, it is not unlikely that counterpressures will arise. Couples will be expected to refrain from reproducing in an effort to keep the number of people relatively stable. As this movement gains momentum, still another major reason for legal unions will be reduced in importance.

A trend clearly visible today is the development of a social arrangement in which a totally emancipated male lives with an equally emancipated female without marriage. This is not to say that thousands of years of cultural evolution, in which matrimony, fatherhood, motherhood, and family life were held sacred, will vanish. But it does appear that those concepts will be altered, so that some of the virtues they were once thought to have will seem like vestiges of an odd custom.

If anyone is skeptical about the prospects described here, he need only look around him.

College students can now live in co-ed dormitories, and they are allowed to have overnight guests of the opposite sex.

Apartment houses are being built and advertised for singles of both sexes.

Birth control information and contraceptive pills and devices are made available at most colleges for female students. A single girl can receive such assistance from most doctors in the community.

Abortion on demand is already available in many states. Following the lead of New York, most others will undoubtedly pattern their own laws after its liberal statute.

Legislation has been passed that gives women legal rights to participate in any activity not specifically requiring a male.

Judging by the unorthodox lives of famous and not so famous persons that are reported in the press, the number of people living together out of wedlock has increased during the last decade.

The question that must be asked is not whether all this will happen, but how far it will go.

Women in Careers

Changes will take place because women have as great a right as men to determine the world's future, and they will participate in business because that area is as much their concern as it is the men's. Since the fear of pregnancy has been removed, companies will be willing to offer more demanding positions to them, and they will have fewer reservations about accepting the responsibility. Moreover, their reluctance to strive for a position because it had been the preserve of men is disappearing. The fear of being considered masculine—the stigma of outperforming men—will vanish from the business scene as ability becomes the predominant criterion of personal worth.

With more women trying for bigger and more important jobs, interfemale competition will sharpen. Female aggressiveness will become keener as women themselves accept the challenge of career growth. Successful career women will be viewed with admiration as more of them are featured in trade and business magazines and papers.

Salary inequities that exist between male and female employees doing the same jobs will be eliminated, both because of social and legal pressure to equalize pay for similar work and because of women's growing influence in policy making as they enter the ranks of top management.

These changes will not take place without repercussions. Perhaps the major problem to be faced is that of the deflated male ego. Many men will find it difficult to concede that a woman is as good an employee at any level as they are. They will be unable to accept women as co-workers.

In addition, complications will arise which are far more serious than that of accommodating a girl jockey in the dressing room. The way in which these problems are solved will have a major impact on the moral and social structure of tomorrow's life. For example, the woman who elects to pursue a career while raising a family will require competent nursery services. The centers for children of working mothers provided by the Soviet Union and the Scandinavian countries may serve as a pattern. Companies may supply this accommodation on their own, as some do today on a small scale. As the need increases, however, the community must fulfill it.

And it is inevitable that the relaxation of parental control which is so noticeable today will receive new impetus. People outside the family will have greater influence on a child, and his beliefs will reflect the attitude which is most strongly imposed upon him. The children of tomorrow may have an even more liberal and less restrictive outlook on life than the young of today. Or it is possible that as the state moves more directly into the affairs of the family, the personal freedoms that are accepted as a part of everyday life will be sharply curtailed.

Another area which will require study is the long-accepted practice in American industry of transferring a man from one locality to another. In the future, consideration will be given to the relative position of the husband in his company compared with that of the wife in hers. Not only might the wife refuse to scuttle her career in favor of her husband's, but it may happen that the man is forced to decide whether he will move to accommodate an advancing wife. Thus problems that are common for married couples in the entertainment field will spread into ordinary lives. Career conflicts will become marital problems—and the decision on what comes first, the home or the career, will be less difficult to make as the ties that once held families and marriages together are weakened.

Management's deliberations on promotions will become far more complex. Candidates will be judged on individual motives, career intentions, family objectives, and the mate's relative position in the household as spouse and competitor. And no doubt many companies will be misled into promoting a woman who tells them that her career comes first, only to find at the critical time that she has decided to have a child or to relocate with her husband. Perhaps this is the most difficult problem that will face managers in their role of evaluating women as career candidates: determining which are truly interested in a total career, which want a partial career, and which are simply looking for husbands. Other women in high-level management positions will be useful in screening candidates and judging their motives.

Sex, Drinking, and Profanity

With the influx of women into career positions, companies will be confronted with new complications not unlike those arising today in social life. There will be an increase in company-generated liaisons when men and women are required, as equals in responsibility, to spend unusually long hours at work. The present secretary-boss relationship has definite limitations:

A dinner during late working hours is acceptable. A late drink to soothe frayed nerves is not; this takes place between supervisors only.

The boss may stay overnight to work out a contract, but secretaries and research assistants go home after their tasks are completed. It is not the practice to have them check into a hotel for the night.

In traveling out of town, only the more avant-garde male executives take their secretaries with them.

Longshoremen's language between men during negotiations and conferences is tolerated, if not welcomed. But as soon as a woman enters, the tone becomes more genteel.

Between themselves, executives share conspiracies that may be barely within the bounds of respectability and legality. But to preserve the facade of correctness, they usually take pains to give a secretary or female administrative assistant an exaggerated justification for what is being done.

Company policies that might have severe repercussions for aged or lower-paid employees are decided upon between men who rationalize their actions with economic semantics. The curt look or reproving manner of secretaries or assistants is ignored as male authority overrides female sensitivity.

All these office conventions will change as women assume

equal standing with men in the decision-making, program-planning, operation-running phases of business. Women managers will make a difference in the lives and conduct of men managers.

Some of the innovations may spell greater danger for our uncertain society. The potential of increased marital discord is real when one considers that in the office a man may spend the greatest part of each day with women, in intimate surroundings, discussing topics of mutual interest. Naturally, not all these topics concern their work. It may follow that the presently frowned upon after-work cocktail, dinner, and overnight stay in town will be to participate in activities other than business.

Trips out of town will inevitably be mixed as women assume new responsibilities. Conferences, business presentations, contract negotiations, marketing sessions, project proposals—indeed, any type of activity that today fills the intercity jetliner with intense men—will have increasing numbers of women participants. No one can expect a company to assume the role of chaperone over its men and women any more than college administrators are expected to perform this chore today. What is significant is that today's college students will make up the next generation of employees.

Discord between a married couple when one of them becomes involved in an office situation that is not acceptable to the other could force companies to urge traveling personnel to use judgment in their conduct. To a remarkable degree, companies today are successful in keeping such problems from becoming more widespread. They accomplish it by having managers of higher responsibility impose their own morality on the people working for them. This will be impossible to do in the future. Any effort to chastise or reprimand a subordinate for conduct that may at present be considered immoral will result in accusations of unfair interference with the private lives of employees. Thus a difficult moral problem will arise in formulating codes of conduct for men and women who spend more time together in very close circumstances as co-workers than they do with their wedded partners.

As for the issue of respectability in language, conditions are changing rapidly. There have always been women who could hold their own with men in bawdy talk. They ranged from the sophisticated lady with the salty tongue to the charwoman type who didn't care who heard her. But until recently, uncouth language was the property of men, between men. The young co-eds of Barnard and Berkeley did much to equalize the use of four-letter words between men and women. Many women may find it desirable to adopt the gutter talk of men to prove their equality. The acceptance of such language could spread into homes where what is now considered forbidden may become the ordinary dinner-table idiom.

The threat exists that in an effort to prove themselves equal, the women of today and tomorrow may acquire men's worst habits. Freedom of participation and action may be interpreted by willing males and misguided females as a license for loose living. If female liberation does come to mean moral anarchy, both men and women will lose far more than either can gain. However, if the right of women to participate fully in all aspects of the world's affairs comes to mean that everyone assumes greater responsibility for a better world, then the removal of the bonds that have held women back is overdue. It is this outcome that managers of today and tomorrow must work for.

Promotion, Not Tokenism

More than most managers recognize, women have been slowly and quietly assuming greater responsibilities. They have been able to do so because their performance was outstanding compared with that of the men they were competing against. The female engineer is accepted; women are successful in advertising; office managers, taxi drivers, heads of government agencies today are often women. They worked hard to receive the recognition, and they are retaining their positions by doing well in them.

As the forces of changing mores and government support for these changes combine to assure equality of treatment for women, there will be real opportunity for advancement, not mere tokenism. Salaries will be based strictly on responsibility and performance, not on sex distinctions. Traditional means of promoting men into positions of authority will not suffice; women will be on a par with men, and gender will be ignored. There will be no glib acceptance of the claim that strength of character, toughness, and rationality are exclusively masculine traits.

This change is long overdue. The picture of the superior man, guardian of the weaker sex, was never real except in the minds of male romanticists. From the beginning of recorded history there have been women who have held their own in comparison with men. Ruth and Salome were important figures in the Bible. Cleopatra and Eleanor of Aquitaine ruled and determined the course of history. Catherine of Russia and Elizabeth of England laid the foundations for modern states. By their lives and their works, George Sand and the Brontës brought about changes in cultural patterns that extend to this day. Marie Curie and Amelia Earhart made major contributions to science and transportation. Eleanor Roosevelt and Frances Perkins participated in civil movements and in government. It may be claimed that by its very brevity, this list of famous names emphasizes the rarity of outstanding women in world affairs. But in fact what it means is that despite the historical tendency to relegate women to the shadows, they have repeatedly been able to overcome all obstacles and make their presence felt.

The manager must be prepared to accept the female in all

phases of his business activity. To do this will require a clear and honest analysis of what company practice has been in the past. Only rarely are there written policies dictating that a "men only" rule is to be followed in making certain promotions; usually the rule is not formalized, though it is strictly applied.

A review of positions held by women will show that their promotion route has been in areas where the supervision of females was the responsibility. There has been an unwritten rule among men that they will not accept supervision from women. By applying this concept over wide areas and by relegating women to particular types of work, management readily came to view it as the natural way of doing things. The fact that this natural order was male-inspired and -enforced was conveniently overlooked. The simple truth is that women, when given the opportunity to engage in open competition with men in any attribute of a desirable employee, have more than held their own.

As for the difference in physical strength between the sexes, very few jobs exist where the exertion required has not been reduced to the capability of the smallest woman. A crane lifting 40 tons may look as if the operator needs brute strength, but in reality a child could maneuver it. Through supplemental power sources, most jobs where physical strength or stamina used to be involved have now been adapted to women's strength.

In mentality, there is no evidence to suggest that girls are less capable than boys. Most men will recall with embarrassment that a number of girls in high school and college performed better than they did. Generally speaking, these girls did better in the humanities and in languages, though there seemed to be a few who excelled in the "male" subjects of mathematics and science. It may be that females lose this capability at a certain point in life, but this is not likely. What seems to happen is that social expectations define what young ladies are to do and are not to do as they mature. In the past, one of the forbidden things was to enter male fields of endeavor.

Will Women Make Changes?

Because of the very characteristics associated with the "woman's viewpoint," the introduction of women into the inner circles of business management may have wonderful consequences. At least, it may until women too have had time to build a tradition of strict adherence to the "profit today" motive. And before then it is to be hoped that the thinking of the managerial-executive community will have evolved toward the concept of coequal business-social returns on investment.

From their experience as consumers, women will be cautious about placing an unsafe or marginal household appliance on the market. Once they are in authoritative positions, they will be able to stop such an action before damage is done either to the buying public or to the company.

The contention that men and women are equal does not mean that they are not different: there is a compassion and depth of feeling in the psyche of the woman that can mitigate against the despoliation of the land. Women's influence is badly needed in a climate of opinion where esthetics and conservation are shunned.

In addition, standards of fairness and justice are less easily compromised by women than by men. Perhaps this stems from women's knowledge that they have been treated less fairly than they should have been over the years. For whatever reason, the mental bribe that men succumb to is less likely to sway the female manager.

Regarding management's fear that some women executives will become sexually involved with their male co-workers, the added feeling of security which a woman acquires from her position will work against this tendency. There will be less need for her to seek a male as a secondary defense when she knows that she can support herself and a family through her own talents. Thus the effect of women's business emancipation might be a strengthening, not a loosening, of sexual morals. Security resulting in confidence may replace the doubt and desperation that sometimes lead to the marital triangle.

Another characteristic of women is their magnificent tendency to be fiscal conservatives. The stereotype of the extravagant woman loading her charge accounts with frivolous purchases is more imagined than real. Women in this country are responsible for the family's major operational expenditures. The fact that food prices have not escalated as rapidly as prices in other areas is a strong indication that the demand side of the formula can be a powerful anti-inflation weapon. The few extravagant purchases that women make are more than counterbalanced by the economic ability they exhibit in most of their spending. Managements that have a tendency to embark on costly and ill-conceived projects may be greatly benefited as the more money-conscious, financially conservative woman participates in corporate decision making.

The moral and emotional strength of women can also contribute to decisions made on executive row. Some men may be surprised at such a statement, especially in the light of women's well-known tendency to express their feelings in tears or other excited outbursts. But men, who are presumably decision-oriented and unemotional in periods of stress, can arrive at bad decisions in an attempt to live up to this image. Having rid herself of emotional pressures, a woman is more capable of applying reason to an issue than a man, who continues to fight his own feelings. It is a rare executive who has not gone to a woman, whether wife or secretary, with a problem and received a straightforward reply which gave him a clue to the solution.

Finally, the presence of women in the company's inner councils may go far toward introducing civilization into what has been described as the jungle, the snake pit, and worse. Having seen the effect of jungle law on fathers and husbands, women can have a moderating influence in the no-holds-barred arena of business. When his performance is being witnessed by women as well as by fascinated and enthralled males, it will be more difficult for a gladiator to go for the jugular of an adversary. Perhaps as women become more familiar with the conference room they may acquire a taste for blood themselves, but this is not very likely. Having seen loved ones battered by managerial combat, their tendency will be to work against carnage.

Because of what women are in themselves, there is much to recommend their acceptance as workers, as managers, and as business leaders.

Black Woman Power

The arguments for giving her equality in business and industry are not confined to the white female; in fact, there is reason to believe that the black woman may have even more to offer in the business world. The white woman has had a relatively protected existence compared with that of the black. While the white girl grew up safe and watched over by parents and police, the black one was frequently left on her own while her mother and father worked, and the police represented not protection but repressive authority.

Too, since the black male has often been unable to qualify for or hold a job in a white-dominated society, the woman in the black household has been required to take a more important role than her white counterpart. She represents stability and authority; she has done what was needed to maintain a degree of sanity in a world perverted by social injustice. Her magnificent achievement is seen in the fact that so far the black protest has been less violent than it might. Despite

Watts, Detroit, and Newark, the black man and woman have shown far more understanding than we have a right to expect.

The manager today must find ways to utilize the tremendous potential of black women. Their capability need not overshadow that of their men; rather, both must be allowed to work and advance as people in a society that is confident enough not to judge a man or woman by the accident of color. The black woman must be given the opportunity to participate in a cooperative effort at making this a better society.

Managers and the Women's Invasion

The entrance of women into the business world in occupations and at job levels they have not formerly approached will present a major challenge to managers.

Disgruntled men will have to be persuaded to recognize and accept the fact of this invasion.

As different standards of conduct become socially acceptable, company policies and procedures in regard to employee behavior both on and off the job will need revision.

Competition between men for advancement will be complicated and intensified as women add their numbers and begin using their own type of persuasion and politicking.

Definitions of what constitutes work that should be restricted to one or the other sex will require close scrutiny. Except for models and singers, there would seem to be very few occupations where the two could not change places.

Wage differentials and special privileges and protection for men will fail as women exhibit their ability to perform on any job given them.

Greater tact will be required until the male tendency to judge females on their looks is replaced by a recognition of individual aptitudes. This recognition will be accelerated as women rise in the organization and begin to express their views on individual qualifications for a position.

If the challenge is great, so too is the reward. Successful assimilation of women into all areas of the workforce will mean that 50 percent of the population can participate in decisions that affect their lives. Up to now, they were unable to have much influence on the course of events.

Women will represent a side of life and reflect a way of thinking that will do much to offset the cold, precise approach that has prevailed in business and industry for so long. Their balanced intelligence, ability to express emotion, and sense of beauty will be a much needed counterpoint to the male's conceited braininess, cold and repressed humanity, and devotion to utilitarianism.

5

The Manager
and Job Security

THE Industrial Revolution ushered in more than the substitution of the machine for manual labor. It also brought unemployment and the threat of poverty. Although hard times did occur in the agrarian civilization that existed before the development of industrial centers, the peasant could at least raise enough food for himself and his family, and his primitive cottage provided them with shelter. Extended drought occasionally caused famine in large areas of the settled world; but those who suffered were the artisan and his helpers in the towns, which depended on farmers for food.

With the industrialization of the world, the vast majority of people became nonagrarian workers who served others in return for food and shelter. This change has had dramatic effects on those who must barter labor for wages, and wages for food and shelter. The breadwinner is extremely concerned about his job and its permanence and fights against any innovation that affects his feeling of security. This was true of the Luddites in England, who destroyed machinery which they insisted was being installed to take away their jobs; it was demonstrated by American coal miners, who initially resisted the use of machinery in the mines; and it is true today of the railroad and flight engineers who demand perpetuation of positions which are scheduled for elimination because of technical advances. Job insecurity has been a major consideration for the worker since he dropped the plow and picked up the wrench.

Management Depersonalized

Until recently the manager was always associated with the organization, and his position was thought as secure as the company itself. Men were selected carefully for managerial rank, and once they were admitted to the circle of those destined to become the future executives, they could feel safe. It would require a serious business reversal or totally unacceptable behavior for a man to be discharged.

This calm and stability characterized executive row until the end of World War II, at which time there was a sudden great demand for managers by expanding companies. Where positions had previously been filled with carefully chosen men (frequently relatives or friends of the owners or operating executives), they were being offered to anyone who could qualify. The swelling ranks of managers in the rapidly growing organizations became less friendly and more impersonal. Individuals who did not belong to the owner's inner circle rose to high positions, and they in turn evaluated men purely on the basis of performance. The personal aspect of management had disappeared.

The growth in company size had a second important result in company ownership. The rapid development of new products created a need for particular talents, and there was an increase in the number of companies that were established to satisfy the demand for these more complex products. Specialists and highly trained men went into business and hired only men who could contribute to their organization's needs and participate in its growth. Competition for such men became intense, and managers moved from one position to another with a rapidity that had been unthinkable only a few years earlier.

As markets became saturated with products and managers, however, sales competition between companies grew fierce. In order to survive, it became necessary for organizations to merge, absorb, acquire, or spin off. Thus a manager who had joined a relatively small growth company often found himself associated with a giant he did not know and perhaps would never have joined, and he was evaluated by men who were only remotely concerned with what he was doing. The company and the manager both were looked upon as nonpersons, as producers of profit. A monthly report, income statement, progress chart, or computer run was used to evaluate their performance. If the figures were favorable, both were doing well. If they were not, both were doing badly. The remedy was to replace the manager with someone who would turn things around as fast as possible. If the replacement did not perform as expected, he too would be supplanted. The conduct of such an operation required that personal feelings be excluded from decision making. The personal aspect of management was to be avoided at all costs.

Executives now found themselves being judged as coldly as factory hands. Performance counted; anything less than an ability to generate profit and outdistance the competition was unsatisfactory. Managers were fired as casually as hourly employees; indeed, since most factory workers were organized, it became easier to get rid of a general manager than a lathe hand.

A Surplus of Managers

This condition will continue and intensify as business adjusts to an economy free of artificial stimulants such as massive defense and space spending. The supply of managers has outrun the demand and, like any other commodity in a free market, must contract.

The managerial market has been further complicated by a number of factors that previously did not affect the executive. Automation, for example, is not restricted to the blue collar worker; executives are faced with similar labor-saving innovations. Computers are taking over more of the routine planning, scheduling, routing, designing, and low-level decision making that had previously been performed by men.

In addition, the already oversupplied labor market will expand at all levels in the future because of the need to absorb a large number of currently marginally employed or unemployed blacks, underprivileged, older people, and women. It is useless to argue that these people should not be admitted into the market in its present state; everyone has a need and a right to be productive. And society cannot afford numbers of unemployed, underemployed, and dissatisfied members.

Consolidations, mergers, and other corporate devices for joining companies together also contribute to the oversupply of both white and blue collar employees. Because overlapping functions in the new corporate entity can be combined and streamlined, a common result is a reduction in the number of managers as well as factory hands.

Since the earliest times, worker output has been studied to find better, easier, and less costly ways of doing things. It is only recently that this approach has been applied to executives. They, no less than the blue collar man, are now being studied and their performance measured against that of other managers, both inside and outside the organization. Thus the methods traditionally applied by the manager to his employees are now being used against him. The worker has had time to adjust to them; the manager is unprepared. Through unionization, workers have developed safeguards against sudden dismissal that include seniority rights, bumping procedures, and bargaining requirements. In many instances these have been very effective in protecting selected groups from unemployment, although in other cases they came too late to help workers caught in the web of change or relocation.

The manager has not had time to become acclimatized to his new role of professional laborer. The result is that numbers of highly educated men who have held positions of responsibility over groups of other highly trained and educated persons are suddenly unemployed and unable to find new jobs. Thus the goal of developing job security for the blue collar employee has expanded to include his co-worker, the executive.

What underlies an employer-employee relationship? Is it the principle that a contract exists between the company and a worker, and that the limit of liability depends upon the contract? If this is so, then the agreement between a company and its hourly employees is covered by a negotiated document, and so long as each performs according to the terms of the contract, there is no argument. An employee is expected to carry out the work detailed in a job description, and he expects to receive an hourly rate plus benefits, including severance pay if work does not exist.

With white collar employees, the situation is somewhat similar. The person in an executive position receives a salary, a vacation, and insurance benefits. He may also be eligible for a bonus, profit sharing, or a stock purchase plan. Severance pay may be defined, and in actual practice the company will frequently exceed those benefits in an attempt to help a discharged manager go from one job to another.

The shortcoming of any monetary payment plan is that it cannot compensate a man for the one ingredient that has, to date, defied measurement: It does not take into account the time he has spent working for the company and developing a skill which is useful in that organization but may be useless elsewhere. No allowance is made for the fact that a company pays for more than talent. When filling a position, a company wants skill combined with a certain age and outlook. It presumably has definite ends in view, such as how and where that ability will be used today and some years from now. When a man who has been tailored to a particular pattern in a company is fired, no provision is made to compensate him for the sudden necessity to fit into a different pattern specified by another company.

The fact is that almost every termination plan has been developed with the idea that no man need stay unemployed if he wants to work. The fallacy of this reasoning is that there never has been a time when every man could find a job of his choosing, in the location he wants, at a time he decides on.

It is true that there have been periods of severe labor shortage, one of which was in the immediate past. What is not recognized is that the price paid to maintain this recent high level of employment may have been too high. Industries were located with little concern for the availability of labor, on the assumption that the wages paid would induce labor to migrate. Engineers, physicists, skilled mechanics, and managers from all fields were lured to Houston, Cape Kennedy, southern California, and other places specializing in defense, space, and electronics. Peripheral service industries such as movers, housebuilders, construction companies, and heat, light, and telephone suppliers had an artificial increase of business in these burgeoning areas. In similar fashion, as the needs of the steel and auto industries grew, people were relocated, disrupting family patterns and stable lives, and placed in congested quarters where they had difficulty adapting. The spiral of costs went upward as this well-paid mass of people bought goods and services. Despite their high incomes, they were unable to save; the artificiality of their jobs was the reflection of an unstable economic condition, and inflation kept ahead of their paychecks.

When the expansion boom in these industries let down, the shock was felt throughout the country. The big spending by their high-income employees was reduced drastically, and service industries were forced to cut back. The effect spread. Sales of automobiles, appliances, and homes tapered off. Industry was forced to adjust to the new conditions, and employees were let go at all levels. The blue or white collar worker who now finds himself in the uncomfortable ranks of the unemployed will soon have a lot of company, if thinking regarding utilization of manpower continues in its present form.

Jobs in Plenty?

There has always been a tendency to consider the existence of a pool of available blue collar workers as being healthy for the economy as a whole. The fact that a good number of them might be living a marginal existence could be excused on the grounds that the overwhelming majority of people benefited. Now, however, the manager is finding out what it is like to be in the pool of the available unemployed. And a growing number of executives will be unable to find work once they have lost their original jobs, because the demand will continue to shrink. Not only must the economy adjust to a less inflationary period, but it must begin to absorb the black manager and the female manager into the managerial workforce.

When the fear of being unemployed did not concern the manager, he had little reason to think about the problem. He considered it his job to negotiate with the union and attempt to belittle the arguments advanced in favor of job security. He could legitimately maintain, for example, that with rare exceptions, any man who wanted a job could have one. Perhaps it would be necessary for the man to accept less skilled work at lower pay, but employment was available if he wanted to work.

In the manager's view, the man who produced was recognized for his efforts and need not fear being let go. The protective device of layoff by seniority that was insisted on by the unions tended to distort this picture. Security then took precedence, compensation and advancement for able individuals were reduced, and the goal of group well-being was substituted.

The manager might concede that opportunity is not uniform throughout the economy, that a given industry might find itself in a shrinking market, as the coal producers did. But he would claim that coal miners who were laid off could find new opportunities if they would relocate—in auto manufacturing centers, for example. He might agree that skills acquired over decades are not necessarily transferable to other industries, but he would maintain that with diligence and application, a man could learn another trade and be as valuable to a new employer as he was to his last. In any event, if a man were laid off because of the elimination of his job, the company would give him a week's notice in lieu of pay, and during that time he should be able to decide what he wanted to do.

The logic of the manager's argument was clear and strong. There was no reason to assume that American industry would not take care of its workers. That it did not do so he conveniently overlooked as pockets of disillusioned unemployed were left in the vacuums created by closed coal mines, relocated weaving mills, discontinued rail yards, exhausted lumber camps, and inefficient small farms. And within otherwise prospering communities, certain groups were finding themselves in similar circumstances. While their neighbors reaped the benefits of a growing economy, numbers of skilled and semiskilled people in various industries suddenly became marginal employees when they were fired from companies where they practiced a trade no longer needed.

While the electronics boom created prosperity around the outskirts of Boston, local workers who had been left behind when the textile mills moved found themselves unable to fit into the job descriptions written for the new industry. Their former skills did not apply, and they were forced to accept low-paying unskilled jobs.

The steelworkers of Bethlehem, Gary, and Pittsburgh, displaced from their jobs by new machinery that did the work of dozens of men and did it better, watched while construction workers prospered, small industry proliferated, and service workers collected premium wages.

Combines, harvesters, shuckers, and innumerable specialized fruit-picking machines made the farms of America the most efficient food producers in the world. But the necessary investment was so great, and the number of acres required to support such machinery so large, that the small farmer could not participate in the new agricultural revolution. Farming became big business, and the small farmer was forced to sell out to the big operator and become a farmhand working for wages and dependent on the demand for his services—exactly like the city dweller. Thousands of formerly independent farmers in the Midwest, South, and Southwest were unemployed while prosperity blossomed for the new owners of giant farms.

The manager's argument that there was sufficient employment for everyone had logic in its favor: there were jobs in plenty. But it did not work in fact: the available jobs were for particular talents in particular parts of the country. Not everyone could take advantage of the opportunities.

The result is that we find ourselves with a unique form of unemployment in which a country that is enjoying unequaled prosperity also harbors millions of economically handicapped people. The probability is that this condition will worsen unless steps are taken to alleviate it. Relief may be in sight because of factors not directly related to the plight of the blue collar unemployed. What happened to the worker over the entire period of industrialization in America is only now happening to the manager. Though he was totally unprepared for it, he is being forced to face it and take steps to alleviate his condition.

Survival of the Fittest

It is not surprising that the executive should find himself in so awkward a position. More than any other professional man, he has championed the concept of rugged individualism and survival of the fittest. Even the physician, that paragon of individual effort and enterprise, was clever enough to protect his career interests through strict control of the number of doctors.

Airline pilots, who as a group earn higher wages than managers, found ways through collective effort to keep control of their occupation. After accepting the role of working-men early in the history of the job, they continued with that status because it served their purposes. Today there are pilots who earn more than chief executives of multimillion-dollar corporations and work a fraction of the time.

The mild professor, who was known for his willingness to work long hours for small wages, quietly moved himself into a position of financial security with tenure by becoming influential in university administration.

The trade unions of the country have taken great pains to control the numbers and types of workers they admit. The result is that many of their members are paid wages that compare favorably with salaries in middle management, while they have job security that the manager does not dream of.

In short, although a great many groups in American business and industry have developed means of achieving job security, the American manager has not, and the results of this failure are evident today. Men who had never lost a job in their lives are being discharged and are not finding new opportunities. If they do get another job, often they cannot adjust to it quickly enough to suit the new management and are fired once again.

There is an uncertainty in today's managerial world different from anything that ever happened before. The changing business climate is creating an environment that is hostile to many of the men called upon to head companies. The directors, who do not recognize the reasons for the change and do not know how to adapt to it, take the most expeditious course: they switch managers. In this game of managerial roulette they hope to find the man with the special know-how that will enable the company to thrive in the new climate.

Their approach is wrong for many reasons. Good men are having their self-confidence destroyed as they lose jobs and attempt to analyze their apparent failure. The remaining managers watch in horrified fascination, wondering when they will receive the fatal summons. They lose faith in the higher echelon of executives and begin to doubt the validity of the whole system. The long-term effects of reducing large groups of highly paid and responsible individuals to insecurity are even worse. Every person has a personal hierarchy of responsibilities, whether he is conscious of it or not. His first concern is for himself and his family, and he must feel satisfied that he has met this responsibility before he can devote his full energy to other activities. While fear can be used occasionally to stimulate individuals to better performance, prolonged periods of fear create ennui and indifference. Instead of intensifying a man's effort, the threat of losing his job frequently has the opposite effect. After seeing heads roll on all sides, managers develop a fatalistic belief that nothing matters, that all is in the laps of the gods. Companies begin to drift. What might have started as healthy competition among employees is suddenly viewed as a duel which only a few will survive.

Once the corps of managers loses faith in a company—which is essentially saying that they no longer believe in themselves—the life of the organization as a productive unit is jeopardized. And the feeling of defeat is transmitted to potential managers: the manager's children and other young people he knows lose interest in entering the field. Having seen the destruction of someone they consider a good man, they have nothing but contempt for business. Many show that attitude today.

Hiring and Firing

There is no question that managers must be measured by performance, and that men who do not measure up must be replaced. A free economic society should have as few restraints as possible, or the concept of freedom is lost. Nevertheless, these principles must be placed in proper perspective.

Frequently the manager who fails at a given job is a man who should never have been given the responsibility in the first place. Those who put him into the position may have felt that it was a potential mistake, yet decided to do it for reasons of expediency. It is possible that the candidate himself knew of his shortcomings but was persuaded to take the assignment. Under those conditions the man did not fail; those who promoted him did. If expediency prevails again and the man is replaced, the new appointment probably has no more chance of success than the first, because the people in charge have not defined their expectations. To hire a man who can do a job, it is necessary to know what is wanted. Then he can be given the responsibility with the clear understanding that if certain objectives are not accomplished by a given date, he will be discharged.

For many reasons a man and a company may find that they are not deriving mutual benefit from their relationship. In such cases he should not be given an internal transfer, even if the only alternative is to fire him. His presence will be a source of embarrassment to all who were connected with his ill-fated venture; his own loss of confidence may be spread throughout the organization; and his successor may find that he is contending with the visible ghost of the man he replaced. When an error has been made in filling a job, the company must be prepared to write it off like any other error in business judgment.

Against all the evidence, many managers continue to believe that a free economy exists in America. Concerned with their own particular phase of a business, they tend to accept the external controls placed upon them as something natural, while they do not recognize the restraints that others work under.

The marketing manager is aware that he must not become involved in price collusion with his competitor or engage in deceitful advertising. The number of suits filed every year by the government reveals a certain lack of compliance with these doctrines, but the principle of governmental surveillance is also universally accepted.

The manufacturing manager knows that he must produce an item that conforms to government-defined specifications. Whether they concern the amount of butter in milk, the purity of packaged foods, the safety of automobiles, or the content of mattresses, there are standards that he must measure up to.

The same holds for advertising, packaging, importing, and exporting. Indeed, almost every phase of business and industry has compulsory regulations.

There are laws defining hours of work and minimum wages, working conditions and safety requirements, parking areas and building codes.

The belief that American business operates in a free economy is a myth. It is important for the manager to be aware of the extent of local, state, and federal control of business, as well as of the limitations imposed by union contracts. Too many executives operate under the misapprehension that except for the bothersome rules which prevent them from doing certain things in their own areas of responsibility, their company is free to do whatever it sees fit. If every firm were to prepare a synopsis of the governmental and union restraints under which it operates, there might be a concerted effort on the part of all managers to halt the erosion of their authority by outside forces. To prevent further inroads, businessmen must find ways to eliminate the socially unacceptable condition of job insecurity. They must work out a solution that reserves to the company the right to put a man on the job best suited for him and to change the man or the job as conditions dictate. But the individual must not be made to bear the burden of bad judgment or poor planning by the company.

Labor: A Factor of Production

In evaluating the performance of an employee, whether he is a laborer or a manager, there are a few considerations worth noting. A man hired for a given position is rarely capable, by himself, of changing a situation from bad to good. The complexity of business today is such that an interface of activities between numbers of people at every level determines the success or failure of an undertaking. Of course it is possible that the man is totally incompetent. Barring such an extreme situation, however, usually an employee merely contributes to the total of a unit's performance. His part in that overall effort should be clearly understood before it is decided that he is doing a poor job and must be replaced.

Too, conditions may arise that are beyond the control of the top management of a company or corporation. A change in consumer wants may occur so unexpectedly that it could not have been foreseen. The entire economy may retrogress and the individual company be engulfed in the general downturn. Too often, managers who are not even remotely connected with a problem are affected by actions instituted to correct it. The arbitrary 5 or 10 percent cut in personnel that is common during times of business stress results in the discharge of many able men.

A person who takes a position in a company takes on an obligation to devote his energies to its profitability and growth. By concentrating on his job he becomes a specialist in its duties, and this tends to make a single-purpose individual of him. He is like a piece of equipment purchased to produce a particular item: so long as that item is needed, the machine is valuable to the company, but if the product is redesigned or discontinued, the machine becomes surplus. Attempts to modify it, as most shop people know, are usually unsatisfactory. The older the machine, the more likely it is to wind up being sold as scrap.

This is analogous to many managers' treatment of their employees, whom they consider nothing more than impersonal inputs to production. The misconception arises because managers have been raised on a brand of economics that has a very fragile foundation. In its terms, labor is blandly included with materials and equipment as ingredients that compose the means of production. By failing to take account of their differences, this economic approach makes it easy to use and dispose of each factor in the equation in like manner. Before any constructive measures can be developed, managers must reevaluate their notions of what labor means to them as employers, as members of society, and as employees themselves.

Labor: Living Participants

It is very useful to reduce people to numbers. A manager can calculate that a certain number of units of labor, applied for a given number of hours, using stated amounts of material, processed with the applicable equipment, will result in a particular output. Assuming that sales projections hold true, it is then possible to forecast a certain profit. The studies of Taylor, Gilbreth, and other leaders of scientific management made immense contributions in helping managers analyze their operations as functional activities and find the most effective method of using labor units. Unfortunately, this approach also taught generations of managers to think of laborers as nothing more than units of economic value, and the same ideas are now being applied to executives.

The formulas used in the past for projecting and measuring performance may still be valid. But in the future, management must devise a parallel set of terms that spell out the human equation. Management which is practiced using economic principles alone is bound to fail, even if a certain amount of attention is given to the so-called "industrial relations" aspect. Picnics, clubs, parties, and protection of employees' safety and health are not enough. Managers must replace their old notions of labor with a new and different philosophy. They must look upon employees as assets whose value cannot be ascertained accurately, as producers with a variable output that is not controlled by the supervisor, as contributors to society, as takers from society, and above all, as individuals with dreams and aspirations. Employees must be viewed as managers view themselves: as living participants in the drama of business and industry.

6

Employment—A Social-Business Contract

Excluding health, no facet of a breadwinner's life is as important to him as job security. Indeed, many men stay in jobs that they know are doing them harm. The laborer inhaling a noxious gas and the coronary-crippled executive work because they feel they must. A materialistically oriented society requires that its members be able to buy the goods and services their station demands of them. They conform or become social outcasts.

Apart from the financial aspect of work, Americans have a psychological dependence on it. Not to work, regardless of one's class or position, is considered unacceptable. This is true despite repeated charges that large groups of Americans prefer to collect welfare rather than work. The overemphasis on paid employment has sent numbers of housewives job hunting because they feel unproductive working at home.

In the rest of the world during America's early years as a nation, people of a certain class were considered to be above things so mundane as work. America had no such tradition, however. Its growth resulted from the hard work of people who had emigrated from their own countries because they were dissatisfied with the establishment. Arriving here unencumbered with the trappings and prejudices of wealth, they proceeded to develop a society different from any other.

In America a person was accepted for his individual abilities and achievements. Apart from the unfortunate prejudice against the black man, this was true regardless of one's religion or birth. Although there have always been visible divisions between the old monied families and the newer entrants to the ranks of the wealthy, such a class distinction is fairly meaningless because of the social mobility in America. The composition of the upper class is constantly changing as some aggressive and successful people enter it while others with waning fortunes leave. It is not an established, protected class structure like those in foreign nations. Thus in this country the possibility of improving one's financial status—and therefore one's social class—is real and challenging.

The same emphasis on individual accomplishment is revealed by the very efforts made to obscure the fact that a son has entered the family business. It also underlies the reasons given by first- and second-generation Americans for not agreeing to special privileges for black people. We made it in this country on our own, they say; let the black show that he has the stuff to do a job and he will be accepted.

One other factor is worth considering in examining Americans' pride of achievement. The man at work, whether he is a laborer or an executive, is engaged in an act which proves his manhood. The American's counterpart to Latin *machismo* is the advancement and financial reward he can show for his work, so that men have a deep personal involvement with their jobs. It is unfortunate that for so long managers at all levels did not recognize and capitalize on the fact of human identification with what they are doing. People *like* to work, and they feel great satisfaction in being members of a productive group. They also take pride in advancement; the man who strives for greater responsibility and authority is following ingrained drives that are independent of financial rewards.

Unemployment in a Work-Centered Society

Naturally, the person who is absorbed in the game of elevating himself through his own efforts is lost when he suddenly finds that he is no longer a player. Part of the trauma of being fired is the fact that the individual and the people in his immediate world have been told that he is not considered adequate for the job. The loss of self-respect can be devastating.

While leaders of business and industry have ignored the sociopsychological aspects of employment, many union leaders have not. Their major effort has been to find ways to insure continuation of employment for their members. They have fought for guaranteed annual wage plans, seniority rights, severance clauses, control over decisions regarding elimination of jobs, and paced reduction of unnecessary occupations. These moves have been only partially successful, since all companies will reduce their workforces when they cannot provide productive employment.

When a company has grown to the point where it dominates a local area, layoffs can result in great hardship. Not only are the discharged workers affected, but local businesses suffer. The failure of managers to carry out long-range planning, based on realistic projections, which takes into account the welfare of the community, state, and nation has contributed to much unnecessary misery and sacrifice. Companies that lure large numbers of employees to locations far from their homes to satisfy a short-term need for labor are no less calloused than the entrepreneurs who built company towns in rapidly exhausted mining and timber areas and then deserted the entire populations.

There must be a better way of dealing with people as employees, and it is up to management to find it. Ironically, managers have not even been able to protect themselves as well as unions do their members. It has been considered below the dignity of men who reach a certain position to rely on anyone or anything for job security except their own wits. That they have been able to rise so high is presumably proof that they can take care of themselves. Yet bankers see nothing inconsistent in joining FDIC or brokers in contributing to the Stock Exchange Emergency Fund, both of which are devices designed to avoid catastrophe during times of economic trouble.

Managers must begin to think of employees as more than extensions of the company toolroom. In European and Japanese businesses, for example, all employees are viewed as permanent members of the firm. The principle underlying this approach is that when a man or woman, whether manager or laborer, enters into employment with a company, both parties have entered into a social-business contract. For its own benefit American management must begin to operate along these lines.

Leaders of industry and business today must give serious and immediate attention to their role as providers of incomes. Current unemployment statistics are only the first warning signs of a future overabundance of people for manufacturing and business, like the overabundance that appeared on farms a few decades back. This depressed employment situation will be compounded by the need to absorb increasing numbers of the young, the underprivileged, older workers, blacks, and females who must be granted entry and permanent status in the workforce.

The reaction of members of these groups to their lack of opportunity, a reaction which has been expressed in sit-ins, demonstrations, and acts of violence and destruction, indicates what can be expected if they are not accepted into the structure of society. Companies, banks, and stores may become armed camps with tightly controlled rules for entrance and exit. At night all property may have to be protected by watchdogs, and armed guards, and exotic electronic devices. It is conceivable that the country may become a series of stockades as the affluent defend themselves against the deprived. If so, this failure of two hundred years of effort to make democracy work will be far more conspicuous than the glitter of chrome, blare of the jukebox, and flash of the neon sign that dominate so much of our life. Business managers must undertake a crash program to prevent what seems like an inevitable collision between those who are outside the mainstream of society and those who benefit from its prosperity The opening skirmishes are already taking place; the major battles must be avoided.

A National Employment Program

The leaders of business must view employment as a national problem rather than the concern of the individual company, so that they can develop common objectives. And since the overall solution will require cooperation of a sort that may have been termed collusion by the government in the past, government agencies must also be involved. Possibly the Justice, Labor, and HEW Departments, which are responsible for gathering most of the statistics upon which business relies, could be used as focal points for development of a national employment policy.

A congress of American labor, business, industry, and government representatives could be held to attack the most important problem facing the nation today: unemployment. The focus would be on the plight of the black, the underprivileged, the young and the old, and the woman, at all levels of skills.

Committees could be created to define specific problems, make preliminary proposals for solutions, and establish a timetable for their implementation. Some of the topics that need study are:

- Unemployment among blacks.
- White unemployment.
- The needs of youth and the aged.
- Female occupational aspirations.
- Industry manpower requirements, geographically and by skills.
- Managerial unemployment, by industry, locations, and disciplines.
- Projected employment requirements.
- Permanent employment contracts.
- Industry employment clearinghouses.

The committees would report back to an elected group of semipermanent representatives of industry. Participating members would be paid, and all other expenses would be met, through assessment of businesses. The permanent representatives would number less than fifty. They would be empowered to hire consultants from universities and to make final recommendations to companies, which would be obligated to follow the proposals or submit the issue to a National Industrial-Business Relations Board. Money to support the NIBRB would be raised by imposing a surtax on all business returns to the Internal Revenue Service. The government would assume the bookkeeping for the organization and would convene and operate the NIBRB as it does the NLRB today. Representatives to the permanent business group would be chosen by agreement among the larger employers —for example, the auto, steel, aluminum, paper, and drug industries. Smaller companies would be represented by local business groups or associations, through state or regional offices.

The initial objective might be a program that would eliminate all unemployment over a ten-year period. Shorter-term goals for specific areas would be developed. Although it would obviously be impossible to eradicate unemployment in some remote hamlet of the Appalachians in a very short time, small-scale subsidized operations could be planned and put into operation within a few years. For example, people in an area that could not hope to be competitive with more industrialized locations could be set to work manufacturing a product to reduce pollution or increase safety that is required industrywide. Each company would receive a share of the production and shoulder a portion of the loss due to inefficiency.

Priority would be given to the problem of eliminating unemployment in cities and industrial centers. Where it was necessary, companies and unions would have to agree to shorter workweeks for some employees, extended vacations, or staggered work periods. Government subsidies would make up a major portion of the pay that employees lost from actions taken to absorb the surplus labor into the workforce. Clearly, the output of the companies involved would also suffer, and the government would adjust the income tax rate in compensation. It is possible, of course, that the taxes realized from the greater number of workers, combined with the drop in welfare payments, might make up for the money the government lost in granting subsidies and tax relief.

When the long-range problems of employment are studied, solutions can be devised that contain measures like these:

Laborers and managers, after having proved themselves over a three- or four-year period, would not be eligible for discharge except under certain conditions. All, of course, could be fired for fraud or dishonesty.

The blue collar man who was found to be a surplus employee because of a change in technology, and who could not be trained for a new job because of personal limitations or the company's inability to absorb him, would not be turned out into the street. If he had devoted more than three years to the firm, it would be required to assume the major cost of paying him a full salary while local employment offices evaluated his capabilities and experience. They would act as his agent in finding him a position that paid a salary equal to his previous one and that required skills compatible with those he possessed. If training were required before he could fill a position, he would receive full pay while qualifying. Disputes as to what constituted equitable pay and a comparable position would be decided by binding arbitration.

Federal welfare agencies would influence decisions on the award of large military and government contracts. A firm that won a competitive bid would receive the contract, but could be instructed to immediately subcontract the work to a higher-bidding company in an impoverished area. The losing company would operate as a subsidiary of the successful bidder and would benefit from the managerial astuteness that went into capturing the contract. In this way the loser would be able to maintain plant capability that is providing employment for local people.

The unemployed in black communities would be assisted through means other than welfare: jobs would be provided directly in industry. The all too frequent subterfuge of insisting upon training in a government school as a step to becoming a productive laborer would be eliminated. The assignment of black men to every industry and business in a given area would avert the evils of adding a large number of untrained men to one or two companies. The rewards could be great: the attitude of rebellious men could change immediately with the feeling that they were useful members of a productive group, with the knowledge that their jobs were not short-term commitments designed to satisfy some political promise, and with the muscle provided by the paycheck at the end of the week. Such a program would do more than untold dollars spent on welfare, training programs, and armed guards to prevent destruction in the ghettos and the surrounding cities.

What is required from the leaders of business and industry is less speechmaking, pontificating, despair, and nostalgia for the past. It is essential that they recognize their role as one with deep social meaning, and that they find ways to fill it.

Fear Is the Stimulus

Despite the false bravado of today's managers, the fact is that fear has become the primary stimulus in getting performance from many of them. It has long been recognized that men do not perform well under continuing uncertainty. An immediate threat may bring a burst of activity as a person attempts to avoid disaster, but a counterreaction sets in as the body strives to return to normalcy. If the fear stimulus continues, the body accepts danger as a way of life and the mind generates an attitude of indifference. Like the peasants walking blankly through the devastated Vietnamese village, the manager who finds that he is under the guns all day becomes apathetic. Often too he turns sullen, attempts to be daring without taking chances, and ends by failing to perform.

Managers know that today they must diversify their knowledge and experience to remain abreast or ahead of their fields, but many find this impossible to do. The pressure to produce results is so great that they have little time even for their families. Because of the crush of everyday work, men are unable to qualify for better positions that open in their organizations, and they are not trained to cope with the new trends that are emerging in their own fields. The introduction of the computer, for example, found most managers unprepared to understand or employ the device. Too often, mathematical models, operations research, linear programming, statistical decision making, and a host of other tools are comprehensible only to younger, newly educated men. The older managers look on—or are told that they are no longer needed—as the young ones move ahead in the company.

During the expansion that occurred in the 1960s as defense and space activities increased, men entered what seemed to be a lucrative and promising field that needed large numbers of managerial specialists. Just as these companies acquired inventories of exotic and high-priced machine tools, so too they created inventories of promising managers. With the downturn in business, they disposed of excess buildings and equipment. The losses sustained were absorbed and reflected in their income statements, but as the factories and offices were eliminated, the men who had staked their careers on the companies have paid a terrible personal price. Since they were dedicated individuals who worked diligently to become specialized, they now find themselves unqualified for the occasional job that requires filling.

What is more, as a result of the wider acceptance of women and blacks, the number of jobs available for these managers will shrink further. The time may not be too distant when complaints will be heard that women and blacks are being given preference over better-trained and more experienced white males to satisfy a quota which has been established by a government agency.

Lifetime Contracts for Managers

It is, of course, a tragedy that managers are responsible for devouring each other. The misfortune is that they were unable to see the signs of trouble ahead. The manager who spent 11 and 12 hours on the job was considered ambitious and was encouraged in his zeal, instead of being questioned about the necessity for overworking. In fact, he must have been overburdened and unwilling to give up some of his chores to others, or else his superiors were compelling him to spend far more time on the job than a union would allow the lowest employee to work. Whatever the reason, his prolonged workday was an indication that he was reacting to fear: fear of creating a competitor if he passed on knowledge, or fear of being fired if he refused to devote his whole life to work. Yet he could not be promoted when the occasion arose because he had not trained a replacement, and because he had been so involved in daily work that he had not trained himself to do more demanding chores.

Companies that hire new college graduates at salaries close to those of managers with experience tell much about themselves as developers of men. It is convenient for top executives to say that the employee is responsible for keeping up with his profession. Too often this is nothing more than an excuse. Whenever executives find that they must search for work to assign to an experienced manager, or must doubt his ability to move ahead, or must conclude that he is incapable of doing a job, they are obligated to determine where *they* have gone wrong in the performance of their duties. The period immediately after a man is given a job is the time to find out whether he can do it. If he cannot, corrective action should be taken before both he and the company are put into a position from which neither can exit gracefully.

In developing a contract for managers, some of the following principles might be considered:

When a manager is hired, both parties should acknowledge that it is a lifetime contract. That it may be broken by one or the other has minimal significance.

Such a contract results in benefits to both parties. The company can expect that the man has dedicated himself to a job not merely to receive an income, but because he is interested in working for an organization that improves with time. If at some point he receives a better job offer, he will weigh this short-term gain against the long-term benefits of staying with a firm in which he has invested his own creative energies. In addition, the relaxed atmosphere that stems from increased job security might yield a bonus in the form of response from men not operating under duress. Their thinking could be attuned to long-term corporate needs rather than to their own immediate goals.

Still, job security would not guarantee job performance. The simple fact is that many men who are assigned to jobs with responsibility will prove unable to carry it. Here are some suggestions for handling this situation.

Assuming that the manager who did the hiring exercised good judgment and intelligence in his evaluation, the company acted in good faith and may have received some benefits from the employee's tenure. He in turn was given the opportunity to move ahead. For whatever reason, it was determined that he was unable to respond to the challenge. Since he has a lifetime contract, either he quits and seeks his fortune elsewhere, or the company notifies him of its intention to dismiss him.

In either case, all company benefits, which include a guarantee of retirement pay at age 60 or 65 that is close to full salary, will remain in force. If the man finds a job on his own, the company that reemploys him will be required to assume the guarantee or to provide benefits equivalent to those he is leaving. The man is free to bargain on salary.

Assuming that it is the company which takes the initiative in terminating his employment, the man will continue to collect pay that is equivalent to his last salary before promotion, or to the salary paid him before he was hired. Like the benefits, this pay will continue until his retirement, unless the company finds him a job with equal pay and responsibility. The job must be in the man's locality or in an area acceptable to him. Should disputes arise as to the equitability of the offer, binding arbitration would resolve the conflict.

It is clear that companies would screen future employees more carefully in order to refrain from becoming welfare agencies for wandering managers. For this reason managers would find their desirability dropping sharply if they became involved in a series of moves. A younger man's temptation to opt for "forced retirement" would be less enticing, since he would restrict himself in his growth and material well-being. Chiseling on the system could be penalized by depriving an offender of all accrued rights and benefits. Income tax reports could be used as a check against violators.

Finding himself free of the worry of sudden unemployment, the manager could respond to his job with new enthusiasm. The tendency to plan and program on the basis of anticipated quick returns could be slowly relaxed, and profits for the future could be given equal consideration with immediate returns. Managers' new-found feeling of security could also produce side benefits to society in the form of healthier men and happier families.

Such a program would be costly, and at first there would be an adjustment as men who had been hired without too much concern for their futures in the organization were reevaluated. A form of manager insurance, paid in part by the manager and in part by the company, would have to be inaugurated. Rates would be based on the firm's record in hiring and keeping managers. This would be a further incentive for the company to hire men it expected to retain, and for managers to choose an organization they were interested in remaining with. The company that did not have such a plan would be required to provide sustaining wages and continued benefits for discharged managers from its own resources.

Total Employment

The country cannot expect to eliminate poverty and want until total employment is achieved. Anything less can only result in a constant battle between those who feel they are being discriminated against and those who are allegedly the discriminators.

That everyone will not be employed at any one time is assured by the nature of man. There will always be those who for some reason are not satisfied with their position, pay, or progress. In their cases, leaving the job will not mean financial disaster, though it may well end in a severe curtailment of their way of life. In every case, however, there will be a job for the man who wants to work. To be sure, this will be a more rigid economy, but it will be developed, controlled, and operated by business and industry, using the facilities of the government for support.

If businessmen fear that cooperation among companies to solve the problems of society borders on socialism, they must face the fact that business and industry will soon be ordered to do things by the government for social reasons. That *is* socialism. There is still time for action, but it must be imaginative and bold. It must accept the total challenge and make meaningful strides in solving the problem. Managers must display, in a field that is alien to them, the qualities that have made them leaders and innovators in business today.

7

Managers and Youth:
A Reconciliation
of Necessity

THE older generation has sold out. If one is past the age of thirty, there are younger people—by definition, under thirty —who insist that he is past reclaim. These children of free expression point to the many faults in his way of life and repudiate it noisily. To many people, this frenetic hostility seems like the tantrums of overgrown children, as if there were something wrong with the maturing mechanism of young men and women today. The bawled slogans, undressing and overdressing, destruction of property, and defiance of authority appear to be the result of lack of discipline in childhood, the sad aftermath of permissive theories of child rearing. Unfortunately, this may be an oversimplification of the trouble with our young people.

In reality, a very small minority of youth is involved in violence on the campus or in the community. The disquieting aspect is that the majority, while shunning the violence, are in deep sympathy with the protest it expresses. Campus disorders, peace demonstrations, civil disobedience, invasions of stockholders' meetings, disruption of campus recruiting, rock festivals, use of marijuana and other drugs, and defiance of parents, police, college officials, clergy—all would have received brief publicity and faded away if great numbers of young people had not supported them.

Rebellion by youth is not new; it is a natural process through which the young clear the way for themselves. They must have more latitude than the older generation wants to give them in order to make their contribution before they, in turn, lose their strength and exuberance. What is abnormal in the uprising of this particular generation is their disregard of the restraints that had been an accepted part of the game. Protest, ridicule of elders, and exasperation with the establishment were timeworn tactics, but the game had been touch football, not hard tackle. Now the rules are ignored, and though all the younger players may not use elbows, knees, and feet, they stand by while others do.

An Unequal Society

To compound the confusion, this generation seems to have less reason for complaining than any other in history. Children graduating from today's high schools are far better educated than previous generations. Their high school diploma makes them eligible for a low-cost college education at most state universities. For the first time in history, the overwhelming majority of young people are largely free from material want: all but the very poor have adequate food, clothing, and shelter. In fact, foreign travel, automobiles, surfboards, high-style clothes, and every form of electronic entertainment are available to almost anyone who puts his mind to it.

But while abundance seems to be the American birthright, the unfortunate reality is that many people are living on a

level below subsistence. Statistics indicate that although there
has been a decrease since 1959 in the number of people classified as poor, about 25 million still fell into this category in
1968. Of special significance is the fact that the concentration
of poverty is greatest among families headed by women,
among nonwhites (about 92 percent of them Negro), and
among people sixty-five and over.[1]

No longer forced to struggle for himself, the middle-class
youth has time to see what is happening around him.
Through the mass media, less fortunate young people can
also measure the gap between what they have and what most
Americans enjoy. Approaching the problem from different an-
gles, the affluent and the deprived reach the same conclusion:
America has created an unequal society of haves and have-
nots.

City slums, air and water pollution, abandoned autos, and
all the other detritus of the affluent society shock the sensibil-
ities of the young. Scientists speak of "dead" lakes and rivers,
"silent" forests, and "visible" air, and the young conclude that
they are inheriting a land despoiled by their elders.

Preaching and Practice

As children, our young people were taught that this is a
peace-loving nation, yet it has been involved in almost continuous combat from the time of their birth. The European
powers, which their textbooks describe as constantly warring
nations, now accuse the United States of being trigger-happy.
Television news broadcasts show American soldiers in acts of
brutality and destructiveness that had always been attributed
only to our enemies. Inevitably it seems to the young that the
government is deceitful and patriotism is hypocrisy.

The already confused young have been called upon to

[1] U.S. Department of Labor, Bureau of Labor Statistics, *Monthly
Labor Review* (May 1970), p. 65.

fight in an unpopular war—and to heighten the insult, those who could afford a college education were exempt from the draft. The falsity of the system that preached equality for all while creating a fighting army of the poor and underprivileged again alienated both the affluent and the deprived.

Together with the political-economic upheaval, a sociocultural revolution has made chaos of traditional mores. The monolithic authority of the Catholic Church has been shattered as nuns and priests leave their orders and marry. Abortion and birth control, subjects that used to be considered too personal for open discussion, are minutely debated and generally endorsed. Courts are plainly confused in attempting to define pornography and obscenity. Bodies are flaunted in defiance of hallowed rules against nudity, and language never before used in respectable society blossoms in print and in movies. These and other changes have demolished the mythical world that children were told they would enter as adults. The surprising fact is that so many have kept their common sense in the confusion.

Unfortunately, other young people have resorted to a drug-induced dismissal of the entire mixed-up scene. The flight of man to the moon has symbolic overtones in their other-worldly escape to euphoria through marijuana, LSD, the amphetamines, and heroin. Bewildered adults feel powerless, and overreact with criticism of everything that does not conform to their own standards. Too, adults overreact to the highly visible and vocal dissidents, while overlooking the silent and thoughtful mass of young people who are simply trying to find their way. An encouraging aspect of the recent campus disorders is that through them all, a decisive majority of students showed stability and purpose. While the parent may question some of his children's actions, he can take comfort from the strength of character with which they weather the storms of the youth movement. Instead of berating himself or his children, he would do well to study the reasons for their dissatisfaction.

The Manager as Villain

To their distress, managers are singled out by their children at home and by leaders at youth gatherings as prime contributors to the ominous condition of the world. For his part the manager feels that he has done well by his family and by society. Certainly America's business and industrial complex, despite its shortcomings, has been an asset not only to stockholders but to the entire community. Judged by living conditions, food, clothing, transportation, education, and the state of the arts, this country is far ahead of all others.

Yet young people feel a great anguish that managers have dodged all other responsibilities except the production imperative. Polluted waterways, dirty air, garbage-strewn landscapes, shoddy merchandise, unsafe household appliances, deceptive advertising and purchasing agreements, vast profits from guns, ammunition, and military aircraft—these are what the young lay at the manager's door. They see blacks and underprivileged whites who need jobs, skilled employees who are discarded because of their age, and capable women who cannot get ahead, and they are revolted that adults call this a free society. They view the executive's expense-account way of life as one more shady technique that the establishment has devised to circumvent the law.

Young people have learned that in hamlets of Appalachia and the South, people live in patchwork houses without running water or sanitary facilities. In the ghetto there are hovels of indescribable filth, rat- and roach-infested, with occupants who have lost energy and will. Some families cannot qualify for free food because they cannot pay the minimal price for food stamps. Meanwhile, surplus stockpiles rot and farmers collect subsidies for keeping acreage out of production. The emerging adult is bewildered that these things exist simultaneously with the affluence he enjoys.

The morally sensitive postadolescent, still under the influence of the dos and don'ts of his upbringing, is besieged with advertising that extols risqué magazines, revealing clothes, and the latest "skin" movies from Europe. Clearly this commercial ballyhoo is aimed at the excitation of sexually developing young people, who can only conclude that it exists because it is good business. They view advertisements which push sex, cigarettes, and liquor as proof that the business and industrial leaders of the country want to sell their goods, not to accept responsibility for social goods.

Seeing the world through such simple eyes, the young can point unerringly to the sources of the world's troubles. Yet much of what they are expressing in their uncomplicated manner has merit, and it is the difficult task of the manager to separate fact from fancy and find ways of opening meaningful discussions with his young critics. After all, he and they have much common ground. Managers would agree that something must be done about polluted waterways, contaminated air, and our chaotic and callous welfare system. Furthermore, the thought of sending his son to fight in the rice paddies of Southeast Asia is not a welcome one to a man who fought there a generation before.

The Manager as Diplomat

The search for solutions will be futile if each side becomes increasingly entrenched, and it is the manager who must keep this from happening. His experience in business negotiations has taught him to be cautious and perceptive when an issue becomes clouded with emotion. The issues involved here are intensely emotional ones for emerging adults partly because the burden of resolving the problems will fall on them. This generation also inherits the awful responsibility of the hydrogen bomb and the necessity for preventing themselves from destroying civilization on earth, even though men have not yet learned how to live in peace.

In any dialogue with the young, the manager must expect

that every issue will become tangled in a multitude of ancillary problems, for the changes that have occurred over the past twenty-five years are too complex to be neatly separated. The manager himself looks at each problem from two viewpoints: that of the citizen and that of the business executive. The discussion here will focus on his role in business and industry.

One of his first concerns as a member of his company's management is with young people as future executives. The theme that the wellsprings of replacement talent for management are drying up, although it is a favorite with journalists, is matter for light reading rather than serious thought. Certainly there do seem to be some gifted students, and presumably executive material, who have become so disillusioned with business that they will never make it a career. But the manager is more concerned with the vast numbers of young people who have always been interested in entering industry and still are. Today this group is hesitant; they fear that the extreme contemporary criticism of business may be true, and that they themselves will become corrupted if they enter management.

The manager must listen to them, search for points of common understanding, and demonstrate that business wrongdoing in the past is being recognized and corrected. He should not be surprised that his critics are exceedingly long on problems but short on solutions, or that solutions which are offered frequently prove impractical. The following illustrations are provided to indicate how the manager might handle his part of a discussion about some of the issues that disturb the young. The main point to communicate is that he accepts each as a problem and is willing to make a rational and honest approach to it.

Water Pollution. According to the young critic, the solution to the problem of dumping contaminants into a body of water is simply to stop it. He overlooks the fact that his parents, friends, and relatives may be dependent upon the factory for their wages. As with many of the problems about which he feels strongly, he either does not grasp the consequences of corrective action or else misunderstands them.

The executive, however, can certainly agree that pollution of a waterway must stop. At the same time he can point out that a sudden end to it would mean severe hardship for the people who would lose their jobs. He can suggest that the best first step is to study what technical procedure is necessary in order to eliminate the condition, and that the second is to analyze what the change will mean in economic terms. The company, the community, and the government can then work out plans for a solution.

It may be that in order to deal with the pollution problem, the company will need tax relief from the government, concessions from the union in wage negotiations, and community support in the form of exemptions from local ordinances. Taking pains to avoid scare tactics, the company can outline to the other groups that are involved the reasons why it needs their support, and the consequences if they should fail to participate. Management should be able to demonstrate that correcting the problem is not simply a matter of company action but a multi-interest effort.

Sometimes when the other groups begin to understand what their own contribution must be, their interest cools rapidly. If this happens the manager's best talents in negotiation and persuasion will be needed, for it is essential that the problem be solved rather than shelved. Later on, the condition will be worse and the obstacles to its correction greater.

Employing Blacks and the Underprivileged. Although the problem of finding employment for unskilled blacks and whites is extremely complex, there are programs which an individual company can develop. In describing these to young managerial aspirants, however, the executive should clearly define the limits of the company's efforts to assimilate untrained personnel: (1) Employees who are currently laid off may have the first claim to job openings. (2) Union contracts may regulate the advancement of employees to higher-paying skills. (3) Union contracts provide that employees with seniority have preference in layoffs. (4) Unskilled personnel cannot be used in a factory process where they might jeopardize their own safety or that of others, might degrade the quality of the product, or might substantially raise production costs.

The company's plan might consist of a specific program, tied in with the corporate twelve-month forecast, that indicates when unskilled blacks and whites will be hired, how many will be recruited, what training will be given, and what outside services will be established (for example, busing, housing subsidies, health services, family counseling, and legal advice). A company cannot hire large groups of former hard-core unemployables without providing auxiliary services in order to retain them as employees. Thus the company's regular personnel must accept the fact that the new workers will be receiving considerably more than an equal share of benefits.

The community may be asked to help by conducting a special bus service and by enforcing housing regulations in areas that had previously ignored them. Inadequate transportation and housing are major deterrents to ghetto residents who want to work, since the first cuts them off from places of employment, while the second makes the mechanics of living too tiring and demoralizing to provide the background for good performance on a job.

Production of War Goods. So far, only producers of the more dramatic instruments of war have been the targets of criticism from the young, but attention will doubtless turn to others in time. Companies involved in arms production should issue a clear statement on their position and be prepared to defend it.

Such a summary of policy might point out that no business firm has the right to determine federal government action, any more than a state does. Nor is any individual or group justified in attempting to change government policy through force or destructive acts. In a democracy, unpopular courses are eventually altered, and a foreign adventure will be abandoned if the majority of people agree that it is wrong. Neither individuals nor companies make these decisions; the president and Congress follow the will of the people as it is expressed by ballot.

A manager may disagree with the course his company has chosen to take on some controversial issue, and he may try to influence management to change its position. If he fails, however, he must implement company policy or leave his job. After the board of directors has discussed the firm's involvement in a government undertaking and has concluded that it is not morally wrong by contemporary standards, no man in the organization should use his position as a podium for preaching against the decision.

Listening to the Young

Occasions for listening to the young and alleviating their fears about business indifference to social problems can be found by the manager who participates in college and high school discussion groups, takes a part-time university teaching job, or appears at church and civic functions that are attended by young people. For many reasons, however, he may not find it easy to listen to them.

It is difficult to be patient with an inarticulate youth who rambles on about his frustrations and uncertainties. The manager expects people to express themselves cogently.

The manager is irritated when young revolutionaries demand change *now—today—*and insist that nothing less will be acceptable to them.

It is difficult to listen seriously to a criticism of company policy by someone who has never even balanced a checkbook.

Many managers resent being pressed for instant solutions to problems that were agreed to by their predecessors, in concurrence with members of the community. The manager may fear that by the simple act of listening, he is giving tacit agreement to the accusations made. Attempts by executives to talk to groups of young people have frequently been met with insults and abuse.

In spite of these difficulties, the manager must recognize that in the coming years he will not be allowed to use his office as a shelter. Not only are the affairs of the company, its products, and its employees his concern, but the community and the lives of those far beyond the confines of his small domain will be important to him. Regulations involving interstate trade will apply not only to the products that pass between states, but also to the use and abuse of the products, the social good or evil that results from them, and their final disposition as their useful life expires. Company activity will be scanned to see both how well it measures up to internal standards of operational excellence and how well it meets the needs of society outside the organizational structure.

Recognizing that he is involved in more than the simple operation of a profit center, the manager can take the initiative in fostering a reconciliation between the company and the skeptical youth of today. More than his critics know, the business executive has been struggling with the same problems that bother the young, and he has been groping toward solutions.

Our young people can clearly see the advantages of American capitalism, but they have been shocked by a series of traumatic events into questioning values that extend into every facet of their existence. It is not surprising that business and industry should receive a share of the blame for what the young see as an abuse of privileges. The manager must accept whatever accountability has accrued through the shortsightedness of others, and must join in developing the means to recover what has been mutilated in our society. Working together, today's and tomorrow's executives can solve the problems confronting business and industry. It will only be done through mutual trust resulting from open and free communications. Patience and understanding can go a long way toward making this a reality.

8

Communications: Getting the Message Across

I⊤ is a rare modern executive who does not have sufficient information to make a decision, for information is king in the business climate of the 1970s. Specialized organizations are paid handsome amounts for information they gather and interpret; publishers turn out volumes of business statistics; consultants are hired and task forces created to explore new ways of solving difficult problems. Computers can store and deliver bits of data in numbers that stagger the imagination. Closed-circuit tie-ins, desk-top readouts, telephone connections, portable extensions, high-speed printers, random and selective access—all are methods by which computers make information available almost as soon as it is generated.

Despite this extraordinary sophistication in handling and using knowledge, wrong and costly decisions are still made in about the same proportion as they ever were. Viewing its mistakes, management assumes that the solution is to collect even more data or to devise even more elaborate techniques of disseminating it. A vicious cycle develops in which more information, delivered more quickly and manipulated with uncanny deftness, again results in bad decisions. A leveling process appears to take place between competing companies whereby they generate the same information which leads them to the same conclusions. This is seen regularly in steel price adjustments, automobile styling, and television programming. No one is able to gain leverage over the others in the battle for survival and growth. The fear of falling behind is their motivation for continual investment in new techniques of information gathering and manipulation.

Men and Machines

However, even the most sophisticated methods for data processing are only tools in the decision-making process. The variable that can give one company an advantage over another in the battle of wits is the personal response of each manager exposed to the information. With the growth of technology has come a decline in this ability to respond. The depersonalization of the managerial relationship has led men to attempt to become machinelike—precise and unemotional in performing their roles—and they fail because this is not their nature. To ignore man's humanity is to overlook the most important factor in the decision-making process, for the strengths and weaknesses of a man cannot be turned off, turned out, or ignored. The basic stuff of pride, fear, desire, greed, ambition, caution, honesty, distrust—everything that makes man different from the machine—can sometimes be masked, but beneath the veneer lives the basic person.

With the growth of technology it was assumed that the computer and the mathematical model would eliminate the human factor from the decision-making equation. Yet humans still had to generate the programs, feed them in, receive the outputs, and manipulate the information in order to arrive at a judgment. Furthermore, while machines could produce recommendations on a course of action, a man had to carry them out. He also had to take responsibility for them, since no machine or mathematical formula can be held accountable for a wrong action. In the final analysis, the manager must accept, modify, or reject the information and recommendations he receives from a machine. He is there to make the decisions and take the blame.

It is necessary, then, to understand the problems the modern manager has in arriving at correct decisions even while he is literally inundated with information. It should not be surprising to find that these are the same problems which confronted the owner of the vineyard in dealing with the cheating steward of Biblical times. Man has changed very little, and the manager of today and tomorrow can profit by taking another look at human nature.

Most companies have inventory, labor, accounts receivable, invoicing, billing, payroll, and time record data stored in a computer. Ordering, planning, and scheduling are triggered by its memory. Project status and progress, cost analyses, engineering efforts, marketing strategies, and even business risks are being evaluated by the electronic wizard. This marvel of the technological age can handle such a quantity of data that a new specialist has arisen: the technician who ascertains what information is pertinent and what is sheer excess. Not only is it economically advisable to be selective because of the high cost of operating a computer, but it is equally important to save the manager's time in analyzing the harvest of information.

Assuming that only pertinent data are fed to and received from the computer, the problem of correctly using them remains. No information, regardless of how voluminous, accurate, or timely, has value in itself. Its worth lies in the use it is put to by men of responsibility; it must be communicated between individuals who understand one another's motives. Unfortunately, the trend toward technology in the practice of management has obscured the place of man in the management role. The result is that the communication problem, instead of being clarified, has become more confused and complex.

In its simplest form, communication is the transmission of information from one station (person, machine, or record) to another. Much more is involved, however, because unless that which is being transmitted has meaning to both sender and receiver, communication does not take place. The generation and transmission of information must follow clear rules that are accepted by sender and receiver, and occasions for changing the rules or the raw data must be eliminated. To participate in effective communications it is necessary to understand what takes place in the act of generating information; what may, and frequently does, happen to frustrate this act; and what can be done to elicit the correct response from the stimulus created by a message.

Transmission, Reception, and Results

Clearly, before communication can begin there must be a basis for understanding between sender and receiver. Once a common ground for the exchange of ideas has been established, it is necessary to define precisely the terms and words used. An American company may agree to purchase prints and specifications of a German-designed machine only to find that it must spend a small fortune translating dimensions from the metric to the English system. When a firm is negotiating to purchase bulk material, is the quantity a "short" ton or the "long" ton? Does stationery come in sheets, reams, or cartons of a given volume? Are suits of clothes short, regular, or long, and are they all the same size? Is a percentage discounted, prorated, compounded, or averaged? On the household level, is the cost of a box of detergent based on weight or volume, net or gross? Is a can of peaches priced on the weight of the peaches, the weight of the peaches and juice, or the number of peaches of a given size? Commissions on standardization are attempting to simplify and clarify these and other such questions.

Even after common terms have been developed, it is necessary to keep alert for the person who misinterprets them. The plant manager may receive a computer runoff on scrap for the month and find that it has suddenly jumped by a factor of two or three. The reason is that where tons had been used to detail certain items on the report, someone has slipped and begun reporting in hundredweights. In another case, someone bases the monthly operating statement on the calendar month instead of the accounting month, and the figures are abruptly better or worse than expected. To communicate—to transmit mutually understood and acceptable information—it is imperative that sender and receiver agree on terms and interpret them correctly.

Communication is not the simple transmittal of information, however; it is the *transmission* and *acceptance* of knowledge *that results in the desired action*. Between the initiation of communication and the time for the desired result, much can happen. Communication occurs only when:

- Commonly understood terms are used.
- Sender and receiver accept and acknowledge the need for, use of, and results from the exchange taking place.
- Sender and receiver trust each other to respect the conditions that have been agreed upon.
- Each does what the other expects him to do as a result of the communication.

Communication Breakdowns

The best results in business, perhaps in all endeavors, grow out of personal integrity as seen and accepted by one's contemporaries. Whatever the contents of a communication, it will be accepted and acted upon only if the communicators have mutual trust. Exercising integrity and establishing rapport are highly complex human achievements, as shown by the following examples of communication breakdowns.

The corporate headquarters of a conglomerate or multidivisional firm sees in the monthly reports of one of its companies a consistent inability to project new business, billings, direct labor, overhead, and cash flow. Despite intense efforts of the consultants from headquarters, the company management can come up with nothing more than, "We have the situation under control as well as we can, but the business we are in is so fluid that it is impossible to project with greater accuracy." The conglomerate's financial statement and projection of earnings and growth more and more assume a fairy tale aspect as accounting stratagems are used to avoid showing swings that are too great in the quarterly report. The success of one division is used to offset the failure of another, and before long, even the manipulators themselves lose track. Finally the chairman of the board is forced by sharp analysts to admit that his managerial group has weaknesses that only recently came to light; hence the recent variations in quarterly reports.

The president of a company, after receiving a call from the head buyer of one of his largest customers, reports back to him that delivery of the needed parts will be made within forty-eight hours. Four days later he tries to explain to the livid buyer that his production man assumed he meant forty-eight working hours, not clock hours. Hell breaks loose in the plant in an effort to satisfy the customer, who has threatened to cancel all other orders.

The general manager, who wants to find out the progress being made in a drive to maintain a low inventory, is given a figure for the value of goods on the shelf. From the yearly inventory audited by the company's public accountants, he finds that this figure was understated by a factor of three. Investigation shows that the production control people had been instructed by marketing to consider material committed but not billed to customers as sold. The accountants refused to accept this judgment, since a purchase contract had not been consummated. An embarrassing discrepancy in information is thus brought to light at the manager's expense.

In projecting sales for the coming quarter, the executive vice-president accepts the marketing manager's forecast, which reports a stable sales picture. What the manager did was to offset a potential loss of business with anticipated sales from a prospective new customer. However, the loss was a reality, since the company had received a cancellation notice, whereas the new business was in the initial stages of negotiation. As it turns out, the negotiations fall through. The vice-president is forced to admit that he and his marketing manager were not communicating.

The progress report from the chief engineer was complete and explicit in all but one detail. Had everything gone well, the "oversight" would not have been noticed. Instead, the breakthrough in design that he anticipated does not materialize, with the result that the new unit cannot be sent to production on schedule. In spite of the company's releases on the product, it is necessary to hold back on procurement and sales activities after the engineering deadline comes and goes. The company is publicly humiliated because a manager took the "success oriented" approach instead of reporting realistically on his team's efforts.

A report is requested, to be delivered "immediately." Based on the reporting manager's past experience, immediately means anything from two weeks to a month. He takes his time and does not have the report ready when it is necessary for the company to make a public statement.

An "optimistic" report is requested, and the manager who prepares it forecasts success where no solution is in sight. The manager who receives it, however, concludes that failure is inevitable under the same circumstances.

The customer thought that delivery meant at his own receiving dock; the producer thought it meant at the producer's shipping platform. The accountants received the impression that the income statement was to be based on the current low rates, whereas management assumed that it would reflect average yearly rates. Marketing somehow did not understand that the new-business projection was not to include anticipated sales from the plant still under construction.

Distrust: The Great Barrier

As the examples in the preceding section demonstrate, transmission of information requires more than simply a common language; there must be acceptance of the meaning and intent of what is being communicated. Nor is this all, for the most critical factor in communication is the relationship that exists between the people exchanging messages. The greatest task in the communications effort is the identification and elimination of the subtle and fear-ridden inhibitions that sabotage the message.

At one time, men worked with one another in the knowledge that they would be together until retirement. They came to understand each other well, and there was little reason to suspect one another of ulterior motives in every routine activity. But the antiseptic atmosphere of the current business environment, created by legislation, by the depersonalization of the new technology, and by the trend toward objectivity that shuns intimacy, has resulted in a different relationship between men. Executives no longer know one another; each is a rival in this success-oriented society. Competence is paramount, and in their effort to excel, men become devious and confuse competence with connivance. In many corporations, to say what he believes or to report what he knows is the beginning of the end of a manager's career. It is not surprising that the glue which holds the communications network together has deteriorated.

Trust between individuals no longer exists; suspicion has replaced it as a mechanism necessary for existence.

Honesty has lost the quality of absoluteness; a little deviousness is always beneficial.

The time is gone when a simple, direct question would bring a straight answer. Instead, the message is received with suspicion and fear:

"He's only trying to hang me."

"Let's see him pick this apart!"

"Another one of his cover-ups."

"Give him exactly what he asks for."

"The last time I ran this down, he questioned me for a week."

"He says it's for a home office survey, but every time we do this there's a cut in indirect personnel."

"I gave him the same information last week. Now he wants it in a different form so he can trip me up."

The person who is asked for information will do his utmost to protect his position, even though the threat is imaginary. The person who needs the information cannot make a correct decision based on what he is given. The result is that both terminals of the communication link suffer.

Lack of rapport between individuals creates an attitude of "me" against "them," them being the company. The person responds to a request by thinking:

"They don't have the slightest concern for us; they only care about profits."

"Headquarters says 'jump,' and he asks how high."

"He hasn't learned we're not in *that* business."

There is no sense of common purpose, and the information that is elicited portrays the transmitter as an embattled defender in a lonely outpost. Unless independent facts are gathered, nothing of value comes to light. The results of such failures in communication are apparent in financial reports, company projections, internal program status reports, delivery commitments, profit statements, and the embarrassed corrections that are later issued (frequently accompanied by a short announcement that an executive has resigned for personal reasons).

Men in managerial positions no longer feel free to express what they think; they tailor their responses to what they assume the questioner wants to hear. If the tone set by top management is that of optimism, then the company line is that the glass is always half full, never half empty. With this approach people have a tendency to ignore serious problems while concentrating on the company's successes. Managers who take a balanced view of the pros and cons of a situation are quickly labeled negative thinkers. Thus pitfalls and unfavorable conditions usually go unreported for fear of criticism.

The "deaf" type of manager is another who encourages misrepresentation. "Do it, but don't tell me about it," he says, indicating that the act is wrong but that he does not have the integrity to stop it. Trust between individuals cannot be developed on a base of intellectual dishonesty. Other executives return a manager's report, saying, "Take it back and rework it to show what I want." The manager, who might hesitate to take a paper clip from the company for personal use, is driven to distort information, perhaps at the cost of millions of dollars to others. The urge to protect company profits, the corporate image, and the company's competitive standing has led many businessmen to do things they would object to under different circumstances.

In place of the easy cynicism that prevails, men must develop a new respect for each other that will enable them to communicate without deceit or distrust.

"This is what *I* think the condition is," should be the report writer's attitude, not "This is what you wanted."

"This should be right on target," is the positive approach, in contrast to the evasive "Everything you asked for is included."

"I think we covered every angle," depicts involvement, compared with the defensive "All your questions were answered."

"I'll stake my next raise on it," reflects a confidence that is missing in the noncommittal "This is the best I could do."

"Looked at from every angle, the best that we can do is—" shows a comprehension of the subject and an integrity that are lacking in "A quick reading shows that—."

Climate for Noncommunication

Because the conditions under which many managers operate today preclude the possibility of communications, increasing numbers of men feel frustrated, indecisive, and disillusioned with the executive life. The pervasive obligation to practice deceit is repulsive to those who know that deviousness is frequently a camouflage for ineptness or uncontrolled ambition. In an effort to confuse a situation, some men make the common language that is necessary for communication purposely vague. The competent manager may be forced to participate in this use of obscurity, but he will not be giving his best.

When people are ignorant of the need, use, or object of information, they will deal with it in such a way that their personal interests are not jeopardized. If they can, they will use it to foster their own aims. When there is no feeling of trust between those exchanging information, the larger needs of the company will take second place to the immediate ones of the individual. The result that is expected to follow the exchange of information is then replaced by a token response, which may cause top management to assume that the information has been acted upon. A problem may thus go uncorrected and become worse than it was before detection. Managers must learn to know and respect one another as men and managers before they can develop the mutual trust which leads to open and frank dialogue, which in turn results in true communication.

9

Man-to-Man Management

THE march of events, bringing a totally new concept in executive relationships, is rapidly eliminating the manager's comfortable feeling that he is a member of a team working for mutual security under the company blanket. His sense of well-being has been replaced by the disconcerting realization that the role assigned to even the highest member of the managerial team may well be given to another, and that this sudden change may have nothing to do with a man's attitude, ability, or performance. The development of computerized operations and statistical controls, coupled with the uncertainties created by conglomerate expansion, spin-offs, and absorption of companies, has resulted in a business climate in which executive turnover is swift and casual.

Tenure and Turnover

Until recently, managers accepted positions with the intention of remaining for a good portion of their working lives, if not their full careers. Today the man entering management accepts a job on the basis of near-term benefits and leaves after short-term accomplishments to seek greater financial or career rewards. The fear of being ostracized by a potential employer has been eliminated; executives at all levels remain in a position for a year or two and either leave or receive their discharge.

The old reluctance to hire a man with a record of short-term job holding has vanished; indeed, it would be incorrect to assume that the manager who has gone from one position to another in a short time is less valuable for this reason. His very exposure to different companies, systems, problems, and methods may well be beneficial to him as an executive. It would also be wrong to conclude that a company does not gain from a good executive's work even when his tenure is short. He may be able to introduce changes or cope with and resolve problems that contribute toward the company's well-being long after he leaves. For himself, he may feel that during his brief stay he gained a new capability or expanded in a desirable dimension.

Still, one must ask why such a man, who is obviously an asset to the firm, does not find conditions suited to his personal long-term objectives. Companies require managerial competence, and once it is obtained, it should not be easily relinquished. How can the company respond to the gifted executive's needs?

It is contended here that discontent in executive ranks can be avoided by practicing man-to-man management. To develop this concept, we shall explore what management means, why many executives are disillusioned, and how a company can make sure that it is fully utilizing the talents of a new manager.

The Art of Management

What is a manager?

This question has been answered in many ways, depending on the kind of managerial job under discussion. If a manager's work consists mainly of presenting his company to others, he is an executive. If he is responsible for having material delivered on schedule, he is a supervisor. If he negotiates to buy and sell products or plant and equipment, he is a businessman. But whatever a manager does, his work is not a cut and dried, impersonal process; there is no management that does not involve a relationship between people. Thus a manager is a person who works with people to reach a common goal. How well he succeeds in achieving that goal defines, in absolute terms, his competence as a manager.

Since management is the art of relating to people, it will remain an art rather than a science so long as people and their lives, attitudes, mentality, feelings, and reactions cannot be programmed mathematically and directed by rote. But as an art, it must utilize scientific tools even as the sculptor utilizes the science of anatomy. A knowledge of psychology, sociology, communications, and anything else that contributes to a better understanding of people helps a man to become a better manager.

To work effectively with his fellow managers, the executive must know their personal goals, their needs, their fears and apprehensions, and their concepts of how they relate to the company. He must be able to develop such understanding without probing into their hidden personal lives, for his concern is with their performance on the job. Performance, however, is related not simply to technical ability but to a man's total personality, and the manager who can establish rapport with people at this level is needed more urgently today than he was during the age of paternalism.

After a long period of growth in power and material prosperity, managers are beginning to question the direction their lives are taking. Material gain at the expense of personal happiness and individual development is no longer satisfying the needs of most men. In addition, a significant change has occurred in the skills required in managerial positions since the rise of the computer and the introduction of operations research into the so-called management sciences. Unless the manager is abreast of baffling innovations, he is termed obsolete. Meanwhile new graduates of business schools are anxious to move into companies and practice the expertise they have recently acquired. Instead of a managerial team striving toward common goals, corporate management may be an armed camp, with the new breed on one side and the establishment on the other. Under such circumstances both are discontented and may leave rather than make a career of internecine warfare. Another serious concern for the executive is the accelerating trend toward merger, absorption, spin-off, and conglomeration, which put an increasing number of managers out of work and contribute to an attitude of cynicism and distrust among all managers.

Finally, even in the most balanced of organizations a man's personal and family life will affect his performance and must be taken into account in evaluating or motivating him as an executive. But it is even more important to judge how much of this knowledge should be shared and to define the bounds of decency. Although the company needs to know the man in its employ, surely his personal life is nobody's business once he does his job satisfactorily. Or is it?

Suppose the company is considering transferring him to another location, giving him a promotion and a raise. The move will have to be made, however, at a critical time in his children's schooling, or at a period when his wife is involved in a project that is important to her. Acceptance or rejection of the transfer may seem a simple decision to the company but could represent a tremendous conflict for the manager, and might lead to a loss for the man, the company, or both.

Suppose that a man with a limiting physical condition which may be temporary or permanent (such as a coronary disease or recurring ulcers) is being considered for a higher position. It is a decision that should not be made without a frank discussion of the effects of the assignment on him, his family, and the company.

Suppose that a man accepts an unwanted assignment because he is afraid to refuse it. Should not the company have been aware of his feelings? Or suppose that an executive pushes himself beyond his ambitions to satisfy a demanding wife. Is this factor unimportant to his superiors? The problem of maintaining an aggressive, performing, and motivated group of managers can be attacked only by managers themselves. It cannot be solved through money, titles, or policy statements, but through the understanding and empathy that is developed by communication resulting from man-to-man management.

Manager–Manager Confrontation

What is proposed in man-to-man management is that one manager sit with another and simply talk, about ideas, feelings, intentions, and observations, on a level at which each knows what the other means as well as what he says. It is the give and take of information which is germane to their interrelationship as comanagers. It is based on respect for a man as a complex individual with a multitude of forces acting upon him, and it is conducted in an atmosphere that is as free of tension, suspicion, and distrust as is possible in a presumably impersonal environment.

Participation in man-to-man management requires that two men sit down at frequent intervals where they will not be disturbed and develop a rapport that allows for the easy exchange of thoughts. Since each individual has his own idiosyncrasies, it is necessary that they learn to know one another well enough to recognize the unspoken signals each uses in communicating feelings and ideas that are not at the verbal level.

Frequent meetings are necessary so that the inevitable changes in character, circumstances, influences, and attitudes can be detected before they reach a point that eliminates the possibility of reaction. Above all, the exchange must be personal and intimate enough to make judgments possible that will have constructive results for the company and the manager. It must be remote enough so that neither manager need fear that the other is participating in his life. While these meetings may well determine a course of action in regard to the relationship between a manager and the company, they should not result in familiarity.

The manager-manager confrontation might be an offshoot of the monthly or bimonthly staff meetings, brainstorming sessions, company reviews, or whatever the gathering is called that discusses company goals and problems. During these meetings the top executive of the group can introduce the idea of man-to-man management, describe its aims and benefits, and allow people to express their fears and doubts about it.

Some managers may see it as a cat-and-mouse game with their supervisor over private aspects of their lives. The top executive can reassure them that the purpose is a relaxed exchange of ideas, free from prying, in order to become better acquainted on a person-to-person level. He can agree that circumstances in a person's life which influence his job will certainly surface; indeed, this is one of the objectives of man-to-man management. But they will be disclosed at the discretion of the participants, not as the result of an inquisition. Other managers may fear that if they express themselves fully on any topic, it will lead to a "big brother" situation, with manager spying on manager. It should not be difficult to point out, however, that situations have a way of becoming known, and that they are usually exaggerated by company gossip. In manager-manager sessions, where each man is involved in a direct confrontation with another, the fear of having gossip leak out of the discussion is greatly reduced. Certainly if the company wanted backstairs information, it could adopt far more insidious fact-finding methods.

Sessions can be scheduled once a month, once every two

weeks, or even once a week if a discordant or pressing situation exists in the organization. They may be held at any time
that is mutually convenient during working hours, or as a
luncheon or dinner conference. They should be unhurried,
taking no less than an hour, with no interruptions permitted.

The range of topics should be wide. The meeting might
start with a discussion on how well the manager is doing in
meeting his departmental goals and objectives, and might
proceed to a report on his yearly evaluation. The two managers might then talk about their vacation plans, the reasons
why another department has failed in some undertaking, and
news of a fellow executive who is on sick leave. The conversation could touch on their children in school, a municipal
project, or a proposed change in company promotion or salary policies. They could discuss the subordinate manager's
absenteeism or tardiness record, his personal goals—short, intermediate, and long range—his frank opinion of his department's performance, and his wife's recent election to a PTA
office. In itself, no one topic may be significant in the manager's relationship to the company, but when placed in proper
perspective, it may be a signal for company action or aban-
donment of a proposed action.

For example, the fact that his son has just made the var-
sity basketball team would not cause a manager to hesitate
about relocating, but if it were coupled with his own election
to the town planning commission, or his wife's unexpired
term as PTA president, both together might make a transfer
very unwelcome at that time. If it were postponed for a few
months, he might have a different attitude toward it.

Or a manager's comment that he is giving up skiing or
hunting could lead to the information that his doctor has advised against continued physical exertion. A forthright exchange on how he feels about assuming more responsibility
could follow.

The information that the company is considering opening
a foreign branch may encourage an ambitious man to study

the language in order to get an edge over competitors. The fact that he and his fellow managers were told about the tentative plan would show them that advancement from within is not only possible but encouraged. This applies to any of the company's future expansion plans, however nebulous they may be. Managers can be encouraged to prepare for growth without being given formal commitments.

Manager-to-manager sessions also provide convenient opportunities for discovering and scotching false rumors. A manager may mention that a great many employees are concerned over a piece of hearsay, and the company can take steps to contradict it.

In an informal conversation between two managers the depth of a man's ambitions can be probed and evaluated. Under certain conditions, it may be reasonable for his superior to outline the limit of his opportunities in his current specialty or perhaps even in the company. Sometimes an understanding of the true situation can destroy ambitions that a manager was channeling in the wrong direction and can lead to a realignment of goals toward real opportunity.

A company which is considering a major change, such as moving from one location to another, may discover during the discussions that a large group of key executives will not accept the change. Much time and money can be saved if the company realizes early that alternate plans should be explored.

Inter- and intradepartmental conflicts can be anticipated and forestalled through man-to-man management. In the privacy of an informal chat, individual managers can express their opinions about others in the company before serious outbursts occur.

Topics that should be discussed at operations or staff meetings are often uncovered in these conversations. Warning signals, faint at first, of serious problems become easy to recognize after a period of this type of management.

Changes in a manager's ambitions and needs may be revealed. The company that has been grooming a man for a bigger job, only to have him refuse the promotion because he has decided to take a government post or go into teaching, might have learned of his intentions if it had provided the proper setting for him to express them.

Does It Make Money?

The one real measure of the value of a company program is its effect on profits. Does man-to-man management show benefits on the bottom line in the profit column? If profits are a direct reflection of the capabilities of the managerial staff —and it is contended here that they are—then the results of man-to-man management can certainly be measured in money.

Some may argue that circumstances beyond the control of managers can adversely affect the fortunes of a company, as when the government ban on the use of cyclamates eliminated a major profit producer in the food industry, or when a sudden change in buying habits left Ford holding the Edsel. Even prosperity may threaten a company that is not prepared for it. When Douglas Aircraft found itself short of cash and resources to deliver a backlog of orders, it was forced to merge with MacDonnell Aircraft to acquire the necessary capital. Unforeseen start-up problems may affect the work of a corporation noted for product quality and respect for schedules. This was the case with Babcock and Wilcox, which found itself unable to deliver orders from its new nuclear boiler plant.

Whatever the reasons, companies that experience difficulty do so because of a failure in management, since it is the job of managers to anticipate trends, needs, wants, and styles. Management, as was stated, is nothing more or less than men working together toward common goals. The first goal of any manager is to assure his company's independent existence as a profit-making operation. If there is any question as to whether independence or profits takes priority, note the vicious battles that ensue when one company or group attempts to take over another. All other activities are put aside, and it is only when corporate survival is certain that the managers return to their efforts at making money. When they do, their quality as a management team soon becomes apparent. It takes astute and farsighted executives to institute programs that improve the company's competitive position, expand its share of the market, diversify its activities, and increase profits, return on investment, and equity.

Managers must be mature enough to recognize their personal abilities and limitations and to hire others who can buttress the areas where they are weak.

They must be farsighted in their thinking and intent on the organization's needs rather than their own ambitions. A company derives the greatest benefit from decisions that result in intermediate and long-range advances, not from short-term gains that enhance a manager's position.

Their outlook must be broad enough to encompass the full scope of their activities. They should not focus on a narrow, parochial phase of the business that they happen to understand thoroughly.

They must see their organization as a satisfier of wants, not a producer of items; the company which makes drill presses is the producer of a means for making holes, not a fabricator of machines.

They must be sensitive to feedback from their customers, not filled with conviction that they know better than the user what he wants.

The company that can measure up to the needs of the marketplace, to the scrutiny of the financial world, and to the competitive situation it finds itself in is the one staffed with managers who can work as a team and solve the problems as they arise. To have a responsive team, the company must constantly regenerate its management corps through recruit-

ing new talent, revitalizing long-service managers, and reacting with sensitivity to the needs and ambitions of its managers, both new and old. No longer is narrow specialization a
satisfactory approach to talent development; a man's total capacity and ambition must be recognized and used. The interface between men, with their areas of friction and disagree-
ment as well as their cooperative and harmonious relationships, must be known and channeled productively.
While it may be convenient to consider the manager apart
from the man, his personal problems and family needs cannot
be ignored if he is to become a vital part of the organization.

The successful manager coordinates his team so that individual conflicts are diverted and people's energy is applied
to constructive endeavors. He capitalizes on individuals'
strengths so that the positive factors in an organization have
a multiplier effect in producing results. He respects a man's
personal life, and avoids invading his privacy. The company
that has managers like this has management in depth. Long
before deficiencies develop, the symptoms of trouble are recognized and corrective action is taken.

Managerial Continuity

One advantage of maintaining a team of growing and contributing managers is the saving in time and money on recruiting personnel. Apart from the obvious costs of
advertising and headhunter fees, hiring a man involves expenditures on travel and relocation. The salary he requires
can upset existing pay patterns and force internal adjustments. Managerial time is lost in interviewing prospects, and
the candidate who is selected needs a costly period of adjustment during which his productivity is far below capabilities.

If a manager who leaves is a long-term employee, it is unwise for management to try and conceal the reasons for his
departure. The truth will out, and the reaction will be worse

if there is conflict between the company line and the explanation he gives to his co-workers over drinks. It takes a long time for the waves of discontent to settle whenever a good manager with long tenure leaves because of disillusionment with the company.

If the manager who resigns is a short-duration employee, the results can be equally bad. The other managers ask themselves what it was that he, with his greater objectivity, saw that they do not. If a number of men have entered and left a job in quick succession, doubts arise about top management's competence. It becomes successively more difficult to persuade a good manager to take the position, and a new man on the job who finds out how many predecessors he has had will not hesitate to leave quickly if he is dissatisfied.

Apart from the disadvantages of managerial turnover, the benefits from developing, maintaining, and expanding a managerial staff under controlled conditions are even more impressive. On a staff that has worked together for some time, each man knows the other and understands his strengths and weaknesses. The supervising manager has learned how to complement the deficiencies of one man with the talents of others. The members of the team are proficient in reading and interpreting each other's statements, and they respond to changing conditions automatically. Nowhere is this more evident than in difficult negotiations, such as labor or production contract meetings, in which the team coordinates its efforts with no need to consult one another.

Every company has a certain body of knowledge that must be learned in depth by its managers, a task which takes time and the development of rapport between men at many levels. Continuity of management is necessary for this process, as it is for establishment of the control which results in a smoothly running organization. The company that has a plan for managerial development, expansion, retention, and utilization will find that its entire operation reflects the plan.

Anything that upsets the harmony and rhythm of a

company's work, whether it be a strike, poor marketing forecasts, a late start-up time, or management unrest and uncertainty, will appear in the profit and loss statement. The company that has high quality management is in the best position to create the harmony which is conducive to profitability. Man-to-man management is one way that the managerial team can be optimized as a working unit.

10

Managerial Concepts in an Era of Change

Just as it is no longer adequate to design, produce, and distribute products without regard for safety, health, quality, or ecology, so the manager who had traditionally been valued for his technical competence alone is becoming obsolescent. He will be replaced by the manager who has sociotechnical knowledge, who retains the profit-conscious approach but adds to it the ability to cope with the demands of an exacting populace.

The new breed of manager will not ignore the computer and the benefits of scientific management, but he will be suspicious of the impersonal approach to business that they permit. He will find ways to combine them with the less precise but more challenging aspect of management which involves working with and for people. He will be as interested in material gain as managers in the past, but he will be aware that factors other than an ability to produce an immediate profit will be used to measure his performance. These include his response to the social problems of poverty, civil rights, environmental pollution, conservation of resources, corruption in government and civic affairs, the spreading octopus of government influence, dope addiction, juvenile delinquency, and the utilization of the labor potential of women, blacks, the aged, and the underprivileged. There will be added emphasis on him as a parent, a husband, and a citizen, so that his contribution in the home and the community will be evaluated as well as his work at the office. He will strive for self-fulfillment and personal development rather than attempting to become the mechanical man of American life.

Crime and Business

The manager's involvement in problems of ecology and unemployment have been discussed; there are others which will become equally pressing in the 1970s. For one, the tendency of business executives to ignore the rising crime rate cannot continue, particularly in view of the evidence that the Mafia has been able to infiltrate and control numbers of businesses. The use of foreign bank accounts, despite some progress in making suspected criminal deposits available for investigation, will continue to enable the gangster to extend his influence into respected corporations. No company can be sure it is free of mob participation so long as underworld members can secretly buy into it. In addition, the contract settlement or negotiating assistance in a company's dealings with the union sometimes comes from the mob, and management usually goes along because the alternative might be a strike or a costly financial settlement.

Crime impinges on business in other ways: with the spread of highjacking, in-plant thefts, and organized robberies of banks and finance offices, employee morale drops and insurance rates and protection costs increase dramatically. Embezzlement and the abuse of company funds and property are rising, but there seems to be a pact among managers not to bring any but the most bizarre cases into court. What the future manager must recognize is that the trend in crimes against business is upward, both because the underworld has discovered that this is a relatively safe area to operate in and because more sophisticated people are becoming aware of how simple it is to steal and avoid detection. In financial districts during the late sixties, for example, well-informed young hoodlums took advantage of the confusion resulting from the introduction of computers and absconded with millions of dollars' worth of securities.

Frequently the plant's pool or numbers game which functions openly despite company regulations is part of a vast gambling operation. The shop steward or "factory lawyer" who runs the racket is allowed to continue by a management afraid to risk creating labor unrest. From such seemingly innocent "sport" corruption can spread to include police protection, loan-sharking, blackmail, and eventual criminal control.

A related problem is the ever-present threat of corruption of government representatives, from the policeman on the beat to an internal revenue agent. The city or county official, who has historically collected a rake-off for doing a favor, is now rivaled by state and federal officials who expect their share for services performed. The spread of bureaucracy can only lead to more of this type of dishonesty. Businessmen have a direct stake in seeing that our officials are trustworthy, for business that operates in an atmosphere of corruption is not free. What is more, the spread of lawlessness can lead to the creation of a stronger central government, unencumbered by the niceties of democracy, that has the force and ruthlessness to eliminate the gangster element.

Both as businessmen and as citizens, managers cannot afford to sit by and expect others to solve the problem of the rising crime rate. They have a responsibility to participate as concerned citizens in the life of their community, to refuse to overlook acts of dishonesty and to report those they discover, and to run their companies free of compromise or involvement with persons of dubious character. They must recognize that whatever takes place outside their factories will in some way infiltrate their operations and involve them.

Drugs and Liquor

Another major social illness that has intruded into the affairs of managers is that of dope. Not too long ago, the closest that an executive came to drugs other than alcohol was in newspaper articles describing a ghetto phenomenon. Then growing numbers of hippies began to capture the spotlight with their endorsement of drugs, and suddenly pushers were discovered in the manager's own community and students in the local high school turned out to be addicts. Fear that his own child might be exposed to drugs or even be taking them brought the problem into the manager's home, if not in reality, at least in haunting possibility.

Now many companies have discovered that significant numbers of newly hired young people use marijuana, LSD, or one of the amphetamines. It is difficult for the untrained person to detect a user, but circumstantial evidence suggests that among groups of new employees, whether they are dropouts, high school graduates, or college graduates, the probability is that some are on dope. The problem is new and alien to the manager. When a case is discovered, he and the industrial relations manager usually have a hasty conference and decide to fire the offender. This serves as a warning to other users that they must take extra precautions to avoid detection, while management tries to forget the incident as a bad dream.

Ignoring the problem, however, may allow a serious condition to develop inside the organization. Not only is the youthful marijuana smoker a candidate for more dangerous drugs, but the user of any drug (including alcohol) on the job is a safety hazard to himself and his co-workers. Drugs impair accuracy of performance, and if the user's work affects the safety of the product, the buyer may be endangered. Moreover, while some of the less potent drugs are within the earnings of almost every employee, escalation to the more powerful ones usually creates money problems that can lead to theft or embezzlement. Finally, mental alertness and speed of response are reduced by every drug. Even those that stimulate the user end by overtaxing his energies and degrading his ability to make balanced judgments.

It is likely that the drug user who is employed obtains his supplies in the factory or office where he works. Since a major part of his active life is spent on the job, the company has an excellent opportunity to help him become rehabilitated. It is important that the threat of dismissal be removed, or else addicts will do everything in their power to avoid detection. If they do, the company is harboring a dangerous underground group whose members are in the process of developing an outlaw mentality.

Understanding, sympathy, and humility are the necessary characteristics for working with people who have become ensnared by either alcohol or drugs. To cope with the problem effectively, lines of communication must be established with social agencies, police departments, and religious organizations. Firing the addict merely creates a civic problem and a latent danger to the company as the discharged employee seeks to satisfy his need and perhaps take revenge on the establishment that has dispossessed him. The future will demand managers who have a deep sense of responsibility toward their community and their fellow men, deep enough to make an executive willing to become actively engaged in what may sometimes be unsavory and distasteful. Such a feeling of involvement, which now seems to have only a peripheral relationship to the job of running an organization, will be an integral part of the managerial function tomorrow.

Owners, Profits, and Social Programs

The initiative for social action will not come from the owners, since stockholder and board measures usually follow study, discussion, and debate, a minor problem that is brought to their attention could easily grow to major proportions. It is the manager who has a broad range of authority, and he is expected to use it. Certainly where a program could have an impact on profits or the corporate image he must first receive approval from the owners, but he should be the initiator because he is the one who is responsible for issues affecting day-to-day operations.

Consequently, managers must furnish the board of directors and the stockholders with outlines for social action and reports on programs that are under way. It has been suggested that any undertaking which would affect profits unfavorably will be rejected out of hand by the owners, but this is an oversimplification of the interests of investors and an insult to them as citizens. Over the years they have shown a remarkable willingness to support a company that is under financial pressure and unlikely to earn a profit in the near future. It is only when they completely lose faith in management that they will not endorse its programs. When it is clear that management knows what it is doing, even the most unsophisticated investor is aware that the surest route to profits is through the resolution of problems that threaten profits.

Moreover, the American investor is as interested as the manager, laborer, and consumer in what happens to the country. There is little evidence to suggest that stockholders are against spending, even at the prospect of lowered earnings, when the expenditure will improve the environment and social conditions. On the contrary, company management usually receives overwhelming support for its proposals at stockholder meetings. Owners recognize their distance from most problems faced by operating people and back the management which shows initiative and competence. In fact, if managers refuse to accept responsibilities of a social origin, the owner-manager relationship could be drastically altered as stockholders act to avoid further government involvement in their enterprises.

Industry Cooperation

In addition to promoting understanding and support for their programs among the stockholders, managers must work toward both intracompany and industry cooperation. Leaders of business must find ways to form joint ventures for social action. The fear of collusion in price setting, division of marketing territories, and production and sales strategy has been so great that legal and extralegal barriers have been erected over the years to prevent cooperation between businessmen. Now, however, ways must be found to inaugurate concerted action for still another common good: the reconciliation of a fragmented society.

To eliminate suspicion by the public and the government that cooperation means collusion, all activities should be conducted in an open manner. There is no need to hold open hearings like a town meeting, where any agitator can disrupt the affair (though an occasional open meeting might be scheduled as a safety valve for everyone, including extremists). In the main, industrial leaders could act through intermediary bodies such as business associations. Topics of common interest could be agreed upon, conferences scheduled, and the press as well as a small number of nonindustrial representatives (for example, delegates from federal and state agencies, universities, and recognized civic groups) invited to attend. Some of the faults and imperfections of the business world would unquestionably be exposed, but at least they could be dealt with by industry leaders rather than by critics conducting unsympathetic and sensational hearings.

Such openness might bring about a change in corporate planning procedures; for example, a planned expansion might have to be made public well ahead of time. Even at the present, however, there are frequently long delays between the announcement of a building program and the actual construction, because expansions are increasingly being scrutinized for their effects on ecology and the environment. The advantage that management thought to gain by a surprise statement is often lost in the months of hearings which follow. The result of announcing its intentions earlier could be a more orderly introduction of company plans to the public, while to the firm it could mean nothing more than a shift in the timing of the release.

Employee Cooperation

Throughout a company, there must be an understanding that management's talk about coming to grips with social problems is genuine. Seminars at all levels can outline the corporate position on pollution, housing, drugs, crime, unemployment, discrimination, and any other problem that may be germane to the operation. Employees' opinions and suggestions should be sought and used as a means of generating total support. The company's past failures to meet particular problems should be acknowledged and explanations given of what is being done about them now. A well-informed workforce is the best prevention for the idle speculation and gossip that can destroy a program before it gets under way.

Members of the organization should become more directly involved in outside affairs. Executives should not be expected to stay on the job far longer than the normal workday; on an hourly basis, many managers are paid little or no more than those they supervise. If the nature of management is such that extra hours must be devoted to the job—a questionable premise at best—then that time should be spent in working on problems that affect a man as a citizen as well as a manager.

The company might have two organization charts: the classical tree that shows levels of authority, and another that describes social involvement. Regular staff meetings might include a community affairs discussion. Larger operations might have a director of community affairs to oversee and coordinate activities.

Responsibility for various areas of interest could be assigned to different managers: Employment of the black, the aged, the underprivileged, the youth, and the female would be the concern of the industrial relations manager. The finance manager would deal with problems of slum clearance, transportation, and education. Drugs and pollution would be the responsibility of the manufacturing manager. Contracts administration and the legal staff would coordinate government welfare activity with company programs. The engineering manager would work on problems of ecology, including noise abatement, safety, and preservation of natural resources.

These men would be expected to represent the interests and activities of the community in which the company is located as well as the affairs of the communities in which they live. Guidelines should be established for their paid time which, including the additional education that might be necessary for participation in community projects, could be roughly 60 to 75 percent work, 15 to 20 percent education, and 10 to 25 percent community activity. Some may object that no company can operate with such a low level of managerial participation. But the point is that soon there may be no companies operating as free enterprises if they do not help to solve the problems that their communities are struggling with.

Managers may find that in some cases they must act as stewards of corporate goals, while in others they must represent the community in opposing the interests of other companies. A colleague may be a comrade-in-arms at the office and an antagonist at home in a dispute over ecological problems. In playing these different roles managers will find that they are broadening their own points of view and extending the base of democracy. The destroyer of our way of life, mob violence, arises when the narrow interests of a given group are imposed upon a reluctant majority. By entering the field of social activity, managers can do much to create new channels of communication between business and society and pave the way for a social approach which considers the interests of both.

In the company that undertakes community activity, there will be a realignment of managerial priorities. The measure of the manager will be his total performance in both operational and social tasks, since the future of the company will depend on its total performance as a corporate and civic entity. Social, community, and family needs will be recognized as real parts of a manager's existence, and promotions will be based as much on overall contribution as on in-plant performance.

Costs of Social Action

The manager must also develop skill in presenting the company's proposals for social action clearly and persuasively to the stockholders, so that they will agree to accept lower rates of return for short periods in the interests of the common good. Perhaps ways can be found to moderate the financial penalty for socially beneficial programs. For example, companies might receive tax benefits on their investment in plant improvements that would correct a public annoyance. Unfortunately, this approach would inevitably give government officialdom the final decision on whether the action is satisfactory, as expensive as the company claims, or even necessary. Mutual insurance programs, similar to that of the New York Stock Exchange for brokerage houses, could be devised to create funds for improvements in the fields of ecology, unemployment, assistance to the underprivileged, dope addiction, and any other socially important activity. Through insurance, the floating of bonds, or the development of a contributory sinking fund, industry could finance and control its own destiny. One or more nonprofit organizations might have to be set up to control the flow of money, but in the long run it might be a far better method than allowing the government to become an overseer of these aspects of business life.

Despite the contentions of some business leaders and economists, ours is far from a free economy. But whatever freedom exists is worth preserving, and this will not be accomplished by businessmen's indifference to the demands that they take greater responsibility. At present, except for a very small minority, Americans consider American industry a great blessing. But the seeds of disenchantment can be seen everywhere: in the objections to continued operation of a mineral processing plant in the Midwest, in public concern over the spoliation of the Everglades in Florida, in protests against destruction of the redwoods of California, and in the public's opposition to the SST which resulted in Congressional defeat.

The American people have had the opportunity to experience material well-being, and they like it. But there is a growing feeling that an awful price is being paid for their superficial luxury. To complicate the problem, those who have not participated in the national affluence want to do so. When they join the mass of Americans who have reached certain levels of well-being, doubtless they too will begin to express dissatisfaction with the personal costs. The man who has gained the upper reaches of his company only to find that he lost a family in the process ends up dissatisfied with his gains. The executive who has given his health to climb to success is prevented from enjoying its rewards because he no longer functions properly.

The principle that a man must be totally dedicated to his work is not only unwise but dishonest. It is unwise for a company to insist that its managers become stereotyped automatons in order to advance, because it will develop a reputation that keeps talented men away. It is dishonest because it supposes that a man is nothing but an expendable commodity in the process of generating a profit. No company will admit that it demands too much of its managers, but promotions and salary increases may make it obvious that the man who is willing to sacrifice everything for his job is the one who receives the rewards. In contrast, the manager who develops the motivated team of people in the organization of tomorrow will reconcile the requirements of the company with the needs of its individual members. Job output will have to be increased so that the confusion of daily activities does not push the more important duties of planning and organizing into evenings and weekends. It will take thinking of a kind different from that which many managers have shown in the past to recognize the desirability of maintaining a healthy home and family life in conjunction with a well-scheduled work effort.

For the large group of people who have entered middle-income status, good living conditions lose some of their allure because of the spoiled environment immediately beyond the fringes of their neighborhoods. Wooded, uninhabited surrounding areas no longer exist, and a drive out to the country involves bumper-to-bumper parkway traffic. Nearby lakes and rivers are open cesspools; fields adjoining them are filled with abandoned automobiles, tin cans and bottles, mattresses, and plastic containers. Although the same people who want to enjoy the scenery are the ones who put the trash there, few of us have not known the frustration of trying to get rid of an unwanted refrigerator, washing machine, or television set. Attempts are being made to induce users to salvage materials by offering money for returned bottles and aluminum cans. At best these efforts are important because they highlight the problem; they make little impression on the acres of debris that remain to be cleaned. And certainly the layers of human and industrial waste lining the bottoms of rivers and lakes will take more than gestures and goodwill to remove.

Consumers are looking to the producers and distributors to develop ways to get rid of products that are no longer useful. The manufacturer will soon be considered insufficiently concerned with the total use of his product if he does not acknowledge responsibility for its final disposition. The costs involved in any plan that attempts to cope with the problem will be considered product improvements and will have to be assumed by the consumer, but it is business leaders who must develop the means for corrective action. The challenge is to design products that can be disposed of more easily and that will not be a blight on the land for generations to come.

Industry also has the responsibility to discover safe and effective insecticides and chemical food additives. The possibility of ghost forests and great areas uninhabited by wildlife is becoming as real as the dead lakes and streams that now exist. It is within the scope of this generation to eliminate wildlife from the forests and to find themselves devoid of animal company except for the city-bred vermin who have shown an ability to survive despite the best efforts of man to destroy them.

The manager will be called upon to learn new ways of operating, ways which are foreign to him as an executive in today's business world, but which relate to the problems that are troubling him today as a person in society. Individually as a manager, and collectively as one of an executive group, he will be required to bring into his business life much that he learns and feels in his personal life. It will be a struggling and kicking new manager that enters tomorrow's world, but he will survive if today's executives are prepared to receive him.

11

Portrait of the
Future Manager

A COMPOSITE picture of the man or woman chosen as a business leader in the next few years would show a person who is as profit-oriented as any Yankee trader. The manager of the future will have an array of new tools to assist him in getting the maximum return on investment, and he will be technically expert in using them. Beyond his business expertise, however, he will have a profound understanding of people and a compassionate approach to the management of human beings. He will be deeply concerned with his fellow workers, both above and below him, his fellow citizens, of any color or creed, and his own family. He will be determined to correct the errors of the past regarding the environment, pollution, and the use of resources, so that his society will be fit to live in.

Computers: Potential versus Actuality

The manager in tomorrow's world will utilize techniques and devices that today are only in the rough stages of development. Chief among them is the computer, which has scarcely begun to reveal its potential. As an exceedingly high-speed, high-volume user and generator of information, this instrument must be programmed by someone with an intimate knowledge of the subject. So far a major problem has been that computer technicians have developed the programs, and as a result vast quantities of paper have been produced which yield little meaningful data. At best the so-called computer specialist can do no more than tell what the computer does and how it goes about accomplishing its task. An intelligent appraisal of particular operations and their unique characteristics is required before the computing device can be fully utilized.

The number of variables that go into even the most elementary business decisions is huge, and their definition is elusive. Moreover, most managers make decisions without the remotest concept of the number of inputs and associations that are involved. The computer uses only that which it is told to use; despite the publicity of early promoters, the gadget is simply incapable of thinking. It can tell when something has gone wrong in its own works to the extent that it can recognize a misapplication of information, but it is helpless when it comes to deciding whether what it has generated has any relevance to the outside world.

Today there is a tendency to look upon the computer as an exotic piece of office equipment. As he does with other machines, the manager feels obligated to know where and for what the gadget will be used, to make a financial justification of sorts, and to turn the operation over to technicians. The computer, however, defies comparison with historical devices. Anthropologists have contended that there is an undiscovered animal between man and the lower primates: the missing link. The computer is the missing link between man and the inanimate world of the machine. It couples human expertise in the most advanced mechanical and electrical technology with the limited knowledge that we have of our own highest function, that of thinking. Man has begotten an offspring that is a technological marvel—but a human cretin. Even at its present early stage of development, however, the computer has tremendous potential for those who know and understand its use. This tool is a storing, computing, comparing device. It can memorize almost unlimited amounts of information and reproduce it with total recall. Because it can store such quantities of information in very little space, its memory is one of the most valuable assets of the computer. The instrument can also compute rapidly and with uncanny accuracy, so that it is unbeatable as a high-speed adding and multiplying machine. Payroll, accounts receivable, and billing functions are being performed by computers with great success.

Besides its fairly mundane storage and arithmetical functions, the computer is a comparing device that has some operations in common with the human brain. The brain accepts sensory inputs at a given instant or actively generates simulated situations and compares them with the body of information stored in the memory. In this way it evaluates problems and decides solutions. Of course, no computer has been designed that can remotely approximate interrelationships which even an undeveloped mind can deal with. Because the computer's ability to make comparisons is limited by the information it has been given and the way it has been programmed, this most promising aspect of computer utilization has lagged behind the other two.

The manager of the future will need to understand the computer and its ability to perform complex operations. As he attempts to evoke semihuman responses from the machine, he must develop an awareness of how humans function and an appreciation for the great scope of human responses, reactions, and impulses. Once he recognizes the limits of the computer's flexibility and evaluative powers, he can make far better use of it.

In programming the machine for management purposes, it

is the individual who has participated in the interrelated functions of communicating, controlling, and supervising who can do the best job. Too frequently, instructions to the computer are incomplete or misleading, and the results are a waste of time. The conclusion drawn by many executives is that the computer is a failure; actually, it is the manager who has failed the computer.

It is fallacious to assume that a person who is unfamiliar with an operation can survey what is being done, integrate what he sees with his knowledge of what the computer can do, and develop a satisfactory program. The computer specialist is the first to admit that he does not understand the workings of the company, and the heads of the various departments quickly volunteer that they know nothing about the computer. Together they attempt to set up programs, but neither contributes sufficiently to solve particular problems. Unless specialists are given adequate time to learn an operation completely, they will usually fail to work out a viable system. The alternative is for the company to hire its own specialists, who can learn the business thoroughly before developing programs. This course is costly because it usually takes more than one person; it is time-wasting because the specialists are duplicating information that exists in the form of experienced personnel, and it is dangerous because the company can lose its investment in money and time if a specialist decides to leave.

Thus the first error in utilizing the potential of a computer is to rely solely on specialists, whether they are employed in house or come from the outside. It is managers who must develop computer know-how. But the second pitfall in computer use is to assume that managers have the insight and training to grasp the multiple factors that are involved in translating human activity into the faultless logic required for machine decision making. Ironically, it is the historical tendency toward technical perfection and evaluation that has bred managers who are incapable of recognizing the human inputs required to develop a program. The manager has been encouraged to become mechanistic in his approach to business, but the computer has been developed with the objective of enabling it to approach man's mental processes in comparing information stored in its memory and arriving at a judgment.

The computer is the single most important innovation in the field of management since the industrial revolution. It has the potential of eventually supplanting many of the functions of middle management. There is a compelling need for managers to learn the limitations and applications of this magnificent piece of gadgetry.

Management Science

Tomorrow's tools that will make the job of managing as sophisticated and technically accurate as medicine, bridge building, or drug manufacture are today only minor curiosities. So far they are used in an exploratory way by a few large organizations, but in the future they will direct companies in their total business behavior. One of these tools is management science, whose more esoteric innovations have been received with skepticism by managers who do not understand the principles on which they are based. As in management's experience with the computer, executives have had to rely upon specialists who do not know the operational aspects of a business. The result has been disappointment, as the following examples demonstrate.

An attempt at using operations research in one company's production control and scheduling function did not succeed because the analyst failed to take account of a supplier's habits. That firm, the sole supplier of a critical part, traditionally delivered late unless it was nagged from the time the order was placed. The schedule delay resulted in a cancelled contract, and the company lost a sizable amount of money.

The central office staff that planned the salesmen's time according to the transportation problem, taken directly out of the linear programming textbook, ignored the fact that the best producer doubled back on his trips to accommodate four of his biggest customers. When the central office insisted on the controlled operation, the salesman left and took his accounts with him.

A consultant on statistical decisions for management developed a contract bid strategy based on previously submitted quotes, trends in the particular market, the effects of inflation on labor and materials, the best field intelligence available on how much money was being allocated by the buyer for the product, and information on the business activity of competitors. The award was lost to one of three low bidders; the consultant's company and two others were significantly higher in price. The fact was that suppliers of a basic ingredient of the product were working on new ways to extract the material which would dramatically reduce the product's cost. The engineering department had not been aware of the progress made on the new process and expressed surprise when the low bid was announced. The consultant had not known about the research and had made no provisions for it in his analysis.

A mathematical model was constructed to simulate the results of introducing a single new product designed to replace a number of old ones. The product was basically similar to those presently sold, but it offered some improvements. According to the analysis, the new item would not increase sales sufficiently to cover the costs of going into production. The idea was shelved, and the older group of products was pushed by the sales department. The company failed to ascertain how many customers would buy the new product even if the old ones stayed on the market. A competitor who did consider this sales question went into production with the same new item and swept the market, for it turned out that buyers were willing to pay a higher price for the improved version.

A brilliant research engineer repeatedly asked to be transferred to another project. His request was rejected again and again, and an attempt was made to show him that his background, interests, and abilities were best applied in the work he was doing. Unable to discuss the problem personally with the industrial psychologist, who was an outside consultant, the industrial relations manager described the case to him over the phone and, irritated by the series of requests, recommended that the man be told to stay where he was or leave. It was his opinion that when the engineer was confronted with the ultimatum, he would see the light and comply. On the basis of the facts the manager presented, the psychologist agreed. The engineer quit.

In all these cases, naïve conclusions were reached by well-meaning but hard-pressed executives who did not test the validity of certain techniques. In the future, managers will be required to be learned in management science methods in order to guide their companies intelligently and profitably.

Managing Individuals

Operations research and the mathematical model approach to management that includes linear programming, statistics, econometrics, probability, matrix algebra, and calculus are at present little more than exercises. A few company staff men and many college professors use them for an unending game of "This is what it would be like." They are right, however, when they claim that such exercises will eventually take much of the guesswork out of decision making. But these techniques will never be applied successfully until those employing them have mastered industrial and business psychology. More accurately, management science users must return to an understanding of man himself.

The attempt by scientific managers to equate men and machines has met with repeated failure, because in their enthusiasm to put man into the mold of technical performance, they have overlooked the other qualities that make him infinitely more complex and versatile than the most intricate equipment. Executives must begin to understand why people act and react as they do, what inhibits and retards some of them, and why that which makes one man fearful and insecure gives another man a challenge and an incentive. Once these personality characteristics are better understood, a new age will open for industry. People will be accepted for what they are: animals with many habitual and machinelike characteristics, yet thinking beings who often act counter to the machine behavior that had been expected of them. For example, although man's primary drive is that of self-preservation, people of all types ignore this need on many occasions. Soldiers in battle, parents protecting their young, and children taking care of their parents may reorder their priorities suddenly at any time. Despite the strong pull of man's animal nature, his will makes him unpredictable.

The characteristics of the human personality—pride, arrogance, humility, ambition, fearfulness, honorableness, dishonesty, and many more—have defied measurement. Because they are exceedingly difficult to analyze, there has been an emphasis on the simpler aspects of man's nature. His tendencies to seek comfort and avoid pain, prefer routine to constant change, value security and avoid risk, delight in praise and dislike criticism, seek power and resent subjugation—all have been used by supervisors in attempts to maximize performance. People's responses to stimuli based on these simple mechanisms are easier to observe than are the results of subtler influences on the personality. It is the subtler ones, however, that can make a positive contribution to man's performance at work.

Stimuli based on fear are useful only as long as they are actively applied, for a person will immediately relax as soon as they are removed. Performance that arises from insecurity depends on negative motivation, which vanishes as soon as the threat disappears. The manager who does not understand this finds that his employees loaf when they are not watched, and he concludes that people work only when someone cracks the whip.

It takes positive motivation derived from the higher needs and aspirations of men to develop the momentum of accomplishment that continues independently of outside pressures. Certainly pressure may be required to achieve a short-term goal when a company must respond to an emergency— delivery of a badly needed item, a contract proposal, a cost reduction, or a competitor's threat. Then a manager may need to cajole and demand work that must be done even though the request is unreasonable. Such pressure must be used sparingly, however, for continued emergencies tend to destroy the effectiveness of an organization.

It is equally important to prevent a highly motivated group from falling into complacency. Man is a creature who is continually changing, constantly reevaluating and replacing his priorities, needs, and wants. Man-to-man management can keep abreast of these changes so that adjustments can be made in the management of individuals. The manager of tomorrow will learn to identify the drives that have highest priority with each of his people and that contribute to the well-being of both the individual and the company. He will detect changes as they occur in people's priorities and adjust his emphasis accordingly. The result will be an organization that has long- as well as short-term motivation and employees who identify their personal ambitions with those of the company.

In external details the man who will be tomorrow's manager will have little to distinguish him from the executive of today. Inwardly, however, he will be a more confident man, one who has come to terms with himself, his contemporaries, and society. He will be competent in a way that present managers are not; he will know the intricate tools that have been invented to help him and will understand their application, limitations, and potential; and he will be able to motivate others through comprehension of the complexities that make up the human personality.

12

Which Way?

In the sixties, man severed his bonds with earth, and a new era began, not unlike the period from 1910 to 1920, when the graceful if artificial Victorian age ended with World War I. On July 1, 1969, the headlong dash of technological advancement suddenly reached a time of reappraisal. The mastery of engineering that came to a climax in a cloud of lunar dust signaled the end of man's need to prove his superiority over the elements. Although man thus showed that he could leave earth temporarily, it was a question whether he could live in peace where he was bound to stay. The voyage to earth's satellite emphasized that we have no refuge; we must somehow find ways to get along with each other on this planet. The seventies will be a period during which the people of all nations either come to terms with one another or, in an orgy of madness, demonstrate that they cannot adapt to the environment they have created.

Man's Survival

Today man is the source of his own greatest danger; although he has learned to dominate every natural threat from the dinosaur to starvation, he has failed to control the forces within himself. As an animal he is weak and defenseless, but he possesses an intellect that has enabled him to survive, multiply, and gain mastery over the planets. It is his mind, too, that has brought him to the threshold of cataclysm—or else to a new frontier. For locked somewhere in his fertile brain are the secrets that enabled primitive man to cooperate with other men, which was imperative to his survival then and essential to it now.

Today it is possible to destroy every living inhabitant in the world by the selective use of atomic weaponry. Moreover, the death of the planet can also be accomplished in ways less dramatic than a giant explosion, and man seems determined to explore them all. Pollution and despoliation of the land, air, and waters may result in a poisoned environment where, like the pelicans and the peregrine falcons, man may not be able to reproduce himself after a generation or two.

With the spreading disaffection of youth, much of it resulting from the spectacle of mature men consecrating themselves to material gain, the prospect of entering adulthood is being viewed with such distaste that the cycle of maturation may become disrupted. Many of today's young people in almost every country in the world refuse to accept responsibility and instead adopt the role of the copout or dropout—the physiological adult who is unwilling to assume the role that society has fashioned for him. Dismissing these acts of withdrawal as adolescent nonsense does not contribute toward eliminating the problem but only further alienates the young. If the trends toward waste and destruction, man's inhumanity to man, and disaffection between the generations continue, it is not inconceivable that a mental malaise could develop that would be as destructive as any physical malady.

The Establishment and the Wierdos

The modern manager must not become identified with the established conservative of every era who is convinced that the old way will eventually withstand all assaults from innovators. Unfortunately, as a social group managers are part of today's establishment, and they feel that supporting a concept promulgated by a minority group (especially if the members have long hair and peculiar clothes) is disloyal to their peers. The thoughtful executive may know that the minority group is right, but he is afraid that to agree with the "wierdos" is to condone them and their methods. By their hesitation to become leaders in reform, executives and the rest of complacent society now find that to follow their conscience on certain issues they must be followers of unsavory characters who did not hesitate to champion unpopular causes. While many executives may oppose the war in Asia, they keep silent because the consensus of the establishment is that critics of the war have shown disdain for authority, and that anyone who supports them is also an extremist. The same holds for issues relating to pollution, ecology, and the underprivileged.

Similarly, executives were aware that the graduates they have been hiring showed a knowledge and a sensitivity that the graduates of fifteen years ago did not possess. They also knew there was unrest in this group which was being manifested in turnover, but they allowed it to continue until the young people decided that management's lack of interest was proof that their criticisms could not be answered. By now the radical elements among the young have mustered enough issues to keep well-meaning businessmen on the defensive. Any corrective measure by business management can be interpreted as confirmation that the charges were correct and that only violent action brings change. To identify with the need for reform is to appear to join forces with advocates of violence.

The establishment, although it knew that drugs were a threat to the weak and unwary, showed little interest in attacking the problem so long as addiction remained a disease of the ghetto. When the disillusioned middle-class young took up drugs, society became officially concerned.

There was adequate evidence that the double standard in evaluating and rewarding women in business was an outmoded concept; the performance of the few women who were able to break through the sex barrier gave sufficient proof. While many executives were aware of this, the pressures for corrective action were not great enough to produce change. Again, managerial response was too sluggish and the business world is being forced to change only because of government action and social agitation.

The Survival of America

While a storm grows around them, managers sit complacently developing new and more objectionable ways to produce and sell products of dubious quality and value. It is as if the executive himself wanted to be a dropout and childishly ignore a problem in hopes of making it disappear. The dissatisfaction that is so obvious is coming not from subversives but from stockholders, consumers, students, educators, legislators, and citizens of all classes and races who are disappointed with what the abundant society has failed to achieve. The movement is being spearheaded by the young, who as tomorrow's leaders seem prepared to make radical changes in the American way of life.

Despite all criticism, our form of government and our economic system are by far the most successful ever established. One could not exist without the other, and they are worth preserving even if we must reevaluate many of the concepts that have been accepted over the years. The young of today are far better educated than their parents were; they have a sophistication about sexual and moral matters unlike anything their elders developed; they are afraid of our unlimited military power and destructive capability; and they are enticed by drugs that were unavailable to the older generation. They must not be abandoned, and they cannot be ignored.

They must be educated in the complexities of corrective action, and their support in perpetuating and improving this society must be secured.

To perform well, people must be free from anxiety; managers must be given assurance that their employment is not a one-way contract that can be canceled overnight. Sudden changes in management owing to mergers or acquisitions, as well as constant transferring of personnel in managerially stable companies, create an atmosphere in which the manager's first concern is to survive.

The stability that will be achieved by developing a more secure workforce of managers and blue collar employees will generate new problems. Ways will have to be found to maintain motivation, and these will come from applying principles that make people want promotions and responsibility rather than making them fear unemployment. Tomorrow's executive will recognize the aspirations of all his employees and create ways for each man to fulfill his own higher needs.

The Full Life

Managers, the stewards of the nation's economic welfare, determine how well the total population lives; yet no one has isolated himself more from the full life than the manager. For too long it was assumed in business that an interest in anything besides managerial technical competence, material well-being, power, and prestige doomed an executive to failure. The result is a stereotype of the businessman as a person unconcerned with anything but profitability in his company and success in his career. Although many executives are patrons of the arts, and many more participate in the cultural affairs of their communities, a great number devote their entire lives to business.

The stereotype of the cold and aloof manager is often real when the manager in question is responsible for evaluating, promoting, motivating, and sometimes firing workers. This is a demanding supervisory function that requires a large measure of isolation in order to be as objective and just as possible. Accurate yardsticks for performance are almost nonexistent, and personal judgment must supplement what criteria are available for making decisions involving people. But there is no reason why business must be conducted in a synthetic and sterile atmosphere; the relationship between men can be close and informal without becoming intimate. And such relationships can provide a far more effective basis for evaluation than the superficial ones in which unreal people perform in an unnatural setting.

A more natural association between managers will result in development of greater respect for one another and better communication between them. Men will have less need to hide their true beliefs and intentions in an atmosphere where each knows his co-worker as a complete person. They will be able to respond to one another as humans rather than as fellow robots who are expected to devote their lives to an equally impersonal organization. Unless managers do learn to work with one another as men rather than machines, there is no hope that they will ever be able to participate in the life of the exacting society that is America today.

The Manager's Survival

Will business leaders be able to meet the demands of tomorrow? Clearly the answer is yes: the challenge will be accepted, and it will result in a major triumph for the manager. There are many reasons for this optimistic conclusion. First, it is increasingly clear to most businessmen that they will cease to exist as managers unless they do respond to the needs of society. With the influence that government agencies now have in the operation of so-called free enterprise, the stage is set for more control unless industry undertakes changes *before* legislators decide they are necessary. Self-preservation, the strongest drive in the animal kingdom, is forcing managers to assume leadership in the new world that is evolving.

The demands being made on the manager today are unique in that immediate response is required, whereas social change used to take place gradually. But in the past or in the future, what is sought remains the same: Security, self-preservation, a sense of participation, a desire for better living conditions—these are the same desires that brought people together on the rugged coast of Greece four thousand years ago, on the mud flats of Paris two thousand years ago, and on the shores of Jamestown three hundred years ago. They produced the Magna Charta, the Declaration of Independence, the Bill of Rights, and the Declaration of the Rights of Man.

There is much greater urgency about these demands today, for time is running out. With the acceleration of technology, the decades and even centuries that used to elapse before an abuse became a hazard have been reduced to months and years. The luxury of watching a problem emerge into sharp focus no longer exists. Within a few years, insecticides have created chain reactions that are causing the extinction of bird, fish, and animal species. Once lost, they can never be recreated. The nuclear bomb has brought the possibility of total extinction for man himself. The rate at which humans are able to generate effluents and contaminate the waters, the land, and the air is increasing exponentially. Masses of people who have been ignored and exploited for centuries are finally breaking out in violence.

Management is in the eye of this great social storm as the group that is most responsible for changing men's aspirations from spiritual values to material ones. The executive today must assume the burden of undoing the mistakes of his predecessors, correcting the faults in his own conduct of business, and creating the climate for a harmonious transfer of responsibility to the coming generations.

He will accomplish this, finally, because the manager is a conscientious worker. He will not be willing to leave as his monument a world of trash-cluttered landscapes, cesspool lakes and rivers, stinking and smouldering mountains of garbage, a smog-darkened atmosphere, fire-charred cities and towns, and a population so divided and distrustful that communities will be armed camps. The rush to accumulate profits and promote selfish interests is, in reality, a throwback to the time when man was emerging from barbarism and found that he did not need his neighbor for survival. Man has not improved much over the years, but today he has an opportunity and a mandate to rectify many of his past errors.

The manager must become even more radical than the wild-eyed firebrand and, with vision that leaves his adversaries dazzled, lead the way in reconstructing society. Rather than destroying, he will build on what exists; instead of inflaming people to violence, he will motivate them to improvement. In place of dividing men, he will unite them in constructive cooperation. He will do these things because he is the best-equipped and -trained for the role. Assuming the leadership in such difficult undertakings is demanding and dangerous, but managers have no choice. They must account for their stewardship of the means of production, even though the definition of that stewardship is being extended. They cannot hide from the assignment; they can only perform to the best of their abilities. As American businessmen, they will perform well.

Index